Guardians of the Celtic Way

Guardians of the Celtic Way

THE PATH TO ARTHURIAN FULFILLMENT

Jill Kelly, Ph.D.

BEAR & COMPANY
ROCHESTER, VERMONT

Bear & Company
One Park Street
Rochester, Vermont 05767
www.InnerTraditions.com

Bear & Company is a division of Inner Traditions International, Inc.

Library of Congress Cataloging-in-Publication Data
Kelly, Jill.
    Guardians of the Celtic way : the path to Arthurian fulfillment / Jill Kelly.
        p. cm.
    ISBN 1-59143-007-0 (pbk.)
    1. Occultism. 2. Spiritual life. 3. Celts—Religion. I. Title.

    BF1411.K45 2003
    133—dc21

                                            2003006502

Printed and bound in the United States at Lake Book Manufacturing, Inc.

10 9 8 7 6 5 4 3 2 1

Text design and layout by Mary Anne Hurhula
This book was typeset in Bembo, with Avenir as a display typeface

DEDICATION

It is the very soft little girl in me who has been severely
wounded in this life. Except for those years when
I was completely shut down, I have been blessed
and privileged to talk with
nature spirits for most my life. I turned to the flower
and tree spirits for solace, particularly during times
when my spirit was intensely coerced by negative sexual
powers. In every instance they held my spirit tenderly and gently.
Teachings always came through that lifted me and led me
to a higher level.

I have the deepest gratitude to all of nature for
Her amazing silent outpouring of love that never wavers, no
matter what we do to Her. She is, has always been, and will
always be my Mother. And Her essence is the living
presence of God, Christ/Magdalene's tender embrace,
adoration, and protection of the inner child. Many, many times
over I would not have survived without it. There are
simply no words to say how strong are my love, devotion,
and willingness to serve Her. My wish and hope is that all inner
children of humanity become healed, so that the full flowering
of love, partnership, and oneness between humanity
and the natural world, Our Mother whom
we have forgotten for so long, can come into fruition
and bloom forever in the sweet perfume of Love's embrace.

Contents

Foreword

It is both an honor and a great privilege for me to be able to introduce this unique book to the world. When Jill Kelly first sent me a copy of the manuscript and I sat down to read it, I was overcome with a sense of awe and wonder. Something deep within me told me that this was a very important work that needed to be read by as many people as possible. It carries a message to the humans of this planet that must be heard, especially at this critical time in our path of spiritual evolution.

To better understand the nature of what you are about to read as well as the source of this information, it is important to view it in the proper context. As to the source of the information in this book, I truly believe that Jill Kelly (referred to throughout the book as its "scribe") is merely the vehicle of its transmission. It is not a work of fiction, nor the ramblings of a wild imagination. I have known Jill for a number of years and have found her to be a very gifted psychotherapist, healer, clairvoyant, and a person of very high moral character and ethics. She has worked long and hard to get to the place of clarity she has achieved, and I have come to trust her intuitive abilities implicitly, especially in recent years. While there is no single psychic or clairvoyant who is 100 percent correct all of the time, I rate Jill very high with regard to the quality of information she "receives" from her inner guidance. Rather than saying that this book was actually written by her, it is more appropriate to say that this book has come "through her," for it was received in a form more akin to "inner dictation" or conscious channeling (not too dissimilar from the way *A Course in Miracles* was "received" by Helen Schuman, another psychotherapist).

Although the book describes the ancient knowledge of the Celtic Way, it's tone and terminology is decidedly Christian in nature, similar to the terminology used throughout *A Course in Miracles.* I feel it is important for the reader to understand the deeper context and meaning behind such terminology because it is a book with a message that needs to be heard, not merely by those of a Christian religious background, but by all the people of this planet.

First, the references to God throughout this book usually intend the Father/Mother/God, or more appropriately, God/Goddess/All That Is. In the ancient Celtic spiritual tradition, one in which all of Nature is celebrated, honored, and worshiped, God is seen from the dual perspective of God and Goddess, representing both the masculine and feminine polarities of the Creator force. This duality can be seen mirrored in many aspects of Nature, such as the Sun representing the Father God aspect and the Moon as Mother Goddess aspect. Of course, the greatest Goddess aspect is Mother Nature herself. It is no coincidence that our living planetary ecosystem is referred to collectively as Gaia, the embodying feminine principle or Goddess of the Earth. While many religions teach of a paternal, fatherly figure of God, others emphasize the feminine Goddess aspect of Creation. In reality, different religious approaches emphasize only a part of a much greater whole, depending upon their historical and cultural orientation.

Another aspect of this book is its reference to the Christ and the Magdalene, often used interchangeably with Father God and Mother Goddess. The terms *Christ* and *Magdalene* do not necessarily refer to specific historical personalities as much as the energy, love, and compassion these individuals came to embody. In truth, a "Christed" being is one who has attained the level of consciousness, sometimes referred to as the Christ Consciousness, from which they are able to express unconditional love to all beings. As such, Buddha, Krishna, Kwan Yin, as well as other prominent spiritual teachers are truly Christed beings as well. In the context of this book, the names Christ and Magdalene are more akin to archetypal energies that represent the highest attainment of unconditional love by the masculine and feminine polarities of consciousness, the highest level, of course, being that of Father God and Mother Goddess. There is an old esoteric axiom, "as above, so below," according to which the principles or structures of the macrocosm are often reflected in the microcosm. For instance, the microcosmic patterns of whirling electrons around the nucleus of each atom in our bodies are strikingly similar to the macrocosmic structure of our solar system, with the planets revolving around the Sun. Similarly, the archetypal energies of the Christ and the Magdalene, or "the holy Father" and "the holy Mother" are mirrored in the varying aspects of God/Goddess/All That Is that the Celtic tradition sees reflected in all of Nature (and Creation in general).

The title of this book, *Guardians of the Celtic Way: The Path to Arthurian Fulfillment,* can be interpreted as a reference to another archetypal energy system, the legend of King Arthur and the knights of the Round Table. King Arthur sought to unite his knights by a chivalric code that placed as high priorities love, honor, and service to the greater good. According to legend, Arthur's knights also set out on a quest to find the Holy Grail, the cup of Christ. Along the way, they came to do battle with many that represented the old ways of pain, fear, and oppression. Seen from an archetypal perspective, King Arthur's knights of the Round Table might be viewed as spiritual warriors who sought to banish pain and fear from "the Kingdom" and to raise up the cup of Christ in celebrating his teachings of unconditional love, forgiveness, and healing. Archetypally speaking, this is the true Arthurian Fulfillment. In a metaphoric sense, the dragons to be slain are our inner fears, our traumas, pain, and suffering that all too many of us still carry with us like ancient wounds, but that still need to be healed by the forces of love.

That having been said, we move on to examine the real message of the book and exactly who or what its higher source is. While the many forms of life that populate this planet are truly amazing in their diversity and complexity, there is an entire system of living beings who remain relatively unknown to the vast majority of humanity. Although there are numerous ancient myths, tales, and legends throughout recorded history that describe this aspect of planetary life, there are few among us in our modern industrialized societies who still take them seriously. To those rare gifted individuals with clairvoyant vision, there is a higher aspect of Nature that is readily apparent, but that usually remains hidden from the rest of us—the "devic kingdom."

The word *deva* is an ancient Sanskrit term that, roughly translated, means "shining one." The devic kingdom refers to the community of higher dimensional beings, often called nature spirits, that actually guide the flow of life energies and creative forces into all living creatures throughout the entire planet. Devas include such things as fairies, gnomes, sylphs, undines, elves, tree spirits, and other seemingly mythical creatures who populate a higher vibrational dimension known as the etheric plane, existing in an energetic frequency just above the vibrations of the physical world. Devas can in range in size from the very small to the very large (some as big as a mountain). The late Geoffrey Hodson was an English clairvoyant whose psychic vision was scientifically validated through numerous experiments—for instance, Hodson could clairvoyantly see and accurately identify which rock among a group of mineral specimens on a table was a radioactive emitter, as verified by a Geiger counter. He wrote a fascinating book called *The Kingdom of the Gods,* and in producing it, he worked with a gifted artist to create beautiful color portraits conveying to the reader the true appearance of many devic beings he encountered in his travels throughout the world. In addition to portraits of devas, Hodson also included pictures and descriptions of a variety of angelic beings as well, many of them healing angels.

The devic and angelic kingdoms are but one facet of a great

spiritual hierarchy of beings who work behind the facade of physical reality, helping to direct the flow of life energies and Creator forces throughout all of Nature. There are devas or overseeing spirits that overshadow or work with each individual species and form of life on the planet. For instance there are butterfly devas, bear devas, dolphin devas, and devic beings for just about any form of life one can imagine, including members of the microbial kingdoms. (There are even overseeing devas for each kind of crystal and mineral within the Earth.) Each animal deva might be thought of as the spirit of an entire species. Ancient native American Indians, among the people of other cultures, frequently paid homage to these spirits in their daily life when harvesting plants for healing or when preparing to hunt animals whose fur would clothe them and whose meat would feed the tribe. They always sought to keep a balance with the spirits of Nature, to honor and respect those beings who gave of their lives so that the greater life of the tribe might flourish.

Among all of these unique spiritual beings who populate the etheric realm of Earth, there are a few special beings who are actually considered "guardians" of the planet. They seek to protect and guard the sanctity of Nature from harm and disruption. Without doubt, they have been troubled by the ecologically unfriendly tactics of many modern industries. But in spite of all that has been done by polluting humans to upset the balance of Nature, including the plunder of the vast riches of the Earth without thinking of the future consequences, it seems that the Christ principle of unconditional love still holds among the many etheric inhabitants of this "peaceable kingdom" in their high regard and noble, loving hopes for humanity.

What you are about to read is, I believe, the channeled transmission of messages from this spiritual kingdom of Nature, and it should be read by all people, everywhere. It is a story of love given and sacrifices made by the various kingdoms of Nature, and of the many gifts they've given humanity with their loving intention of helping us in our (too often) silent pain and suffering. Throughout this book you will read messages from not only the devic kingdom, but also from the flowers and trees, the animal kingdom, birds, fish, insects, and even the mineral kingdom of the Earth, all addressed to humankind. It is, quite literally, a kind of clarion call from the many aspects of Nature speaking in unison, directly to us, for perhaps the first time. Although information of this kind has appeared in other channeled sources, I believe the messages herein, cloaked in a kind of Celtic archetypal terminology, are quite unique. Within the pages of this text are not only hopeful messages from the spirits of Nature but also guides to new healing aspects of the plant kingdom (with regard to specific vibrational essences from flowers and trees).

Within the myths of ancient Atlantis and Lemuria, it is said that humans once walked alongside the devas and the spirits of Nature, for people in those days had the natural gifts of clairvoyant and clairaudient perception. It was thought to be a time when humans co-created with the forces and spirits of Nature, often for healing purposes (but sometimes with destructive purposes and outcomes). It is rumored that Atlantis was destroyed because people misused these forces of Nature for purposes other than love and healing. It might be said that their Karma eventually came back to them amplified a millionfold. While the tale of Atlantis is thought by many to be mostly myth and legend, it is still an important parable about reaping what we sow as well as the ability that we have to work cooperatively again with the spiritual forces of Nature. The nearly apocryphal stories of the Findhorn Garden in Findhorn, Scotland, and the more recent Perelandra Gardens of Michaelle Small Wright in Virginia, stand as modern-day testaments that demonstrate how humans acting in cooperation with the devic kingdom can sometimes work miracles in growing tremendous flowers and enormous vegetables in spite of barren, sandy soil and poor agricultural conditions.

It might be said that humanity is finally reaching a level of spiritual maturity when, collectively, we just might be ready to hear the loving messages of Nature and of the Creator, without cynicism or ridicule. If the messages herein are to be believed, then all the forces of Nature and even the God/Goddess/All That Is wish us to succeed in our spiritual quest for love, healing, enlightenment, and an under-standing of the interconnectedness of all beings everywhere. For indeed, the power of unconditional love may be the most powerful healing force in the universe. May it guide each of us along our own individual paths to find the final Arthurian fulfillment.

RICHARD GERBER, M.D.
AUTHOR OF *VIBRATIONAL MEDICINE*

Introduction
My Own Love

The Arthurian legends have always held a fascination for me. As a child I wrapped myself up in my silver-blue satin puff and imagined a prince who would come and take me away to love me forever. That was a dream that I know now was meant to come true, for myself and for everyone on this planet. I have always had a wonder of Celtic ways, the lore and divination, the fine details of archaeological research—the ancient stone barrows and circles that held secrets I could sense but could not reach. I had no idea at the outset that my path of experience and inner teachings would turn the old written druid lessons inside out.

This book came to me in one winter's writing after a long and intensive spiritual climb. I worked for years with the Ogham symbols, inner druid guides, and the trees near my home as I faced my inner fears and kept to a meditative clearing practice, a simple practice but not an easy accomplishment, for these fears had to be lived and experienced in my daily life on an ongoing basis. This demanded perseverance, courage, and, most important, the help of inner guides and teachers who ranged from the Christ/Magdalene to various individual nature spirit forms and forces. It has been an honor and a delight for me to get to know so many of these devic/djinn beings along the way, and I am more grateful than I can say for the heartfelt support and sustenance all of them gave, just for the asking. Truly, the spirit world is most generous, for it has poured out love and wisdom for me countless times during these years of journeying.

I am most thankful, also, to Dr. Richard Gerber for his kindness, gentle support, and friendship in helping me with my own process and with publishing this book. Thanks goes as well to Donna for her gentle willingness to type and create graphics. And I wish to thank my spirit "crew," those who were with me daily these past few years: Sebhaun, Angelica, and Tantra (angelic); Iriseem and Sebhia (devic); and Donardin (djinn); plus my spirit beloved, Firinn (djinn). I send special thanks to the angels Metatron and Gabriel and to Divine Mother and Father who came with such startling radiance at the beginning to start me on my way.

There is One whom I feel closest to and to whom I am deeply grateful, far beyond my words to convey. This is the Christ Presence who came and held me in my sufferings and the painful trials of my wisdom climb. The gentle tenderness of This One fills my heart daily and has answered every plea with abundant strength, common sense advice, solutions that miraculously worked, and, most of all, with a sweet outpouring of love that kept me going when I needed it most.

I wish to say a word about both gender and the use of Christian terminology here. This Presence, who has been my constant guide and companion, has always felt quite feminine to me. And so I acknowledge this with both the traditional masculine and the less orthodox feminine aspects. The names I use were given to me by the Presences themselves, Christ for the masculine, Magdalene for the feminine. I have no wish to offend or force my beliefs onto anyone else. Let each person's own experience of spirit be his or her guide. This book is as accurate a reflection of mine as I am capable of giving. Also, I feel strongly that all spiritual traditions speak of and lead to the same

God/Goddess. There is only One. Each tradition chooses a name to refer to the One, and this is good, for I believe each person's inner spiritual life and guides are sacred above all else. Please do not be put off by names here; just substitute your own.

A brief history may help to place this work within a useful context. I am a clinical psychologist and worked as a therapist from 1976 through 1999. Since then, I have been writing or giving workshops and presentations. I am also the mother of three grown daughters. I have been greatly blessed with the privilege of being with many troubled hearts as they walked their journeys of life. I honor and bless everyone it has been my fortune to know, to serve, to care about, and to learn from. I keep many in my prayers still. But my deepest gratitude goes to my daughters, for the privilege of being their mother has been the greatest joy of my life.

The past six years have marked accelerated growth and spiritual change for me that have come as the result of a commitment I made to Christ to clear all inner fear-based beliefs, to return to love 100 percent and fully purify myself. I learned to access and read energies in 1996 and, with inner guidance, developed a simple method to clear any fear or negativity by visualizing it moving into the bright light in my deep heart and there melting into love. I have made this a daily practice for the past five and a half years.

The result has been a steady and straight path of change on which I have faced fears as they have appeared in my life, persevered in my clearing practice despite great obstacles, and held fast to Christ. It has not been an easy journey; the inner fears are ancient and deep. But it has brought me into a spiritual warriorship, a gradual self-empowerment in the face of darkness, a slowly emerging self-love, and a deep and abiding love of the Christ/Magdalene in All.

Perhaps the most delightful part of this journey has been my intimate acquaintance with a wide variety of nature spirits: from beetles and dragonflies, trees and rivers and flowers of all descriptions to the clothing, cooking, and home devas and djinns who have helped me constantly. They have appeared unexpectedly in my daily life for several years now, sharing their wisdom, their boundless joy (especially grasshoppers!), and their devotion to the All (all forms in all worlds, the One Body of Christ/Magdalene). Their humor, loving partnerships based in sacred sexual unions, and irrepressible love have lifted me and taught me time and time again.

While I channeled the voice of the Guardians coming through in the overall text (set my own self aside and listened and wrote as quickly as I could), I heard the individual voices of the specific deva and djinn who create a single form when I focused on an individual tree or plant or other single form. On occasion, for instance, it was the group voice of trees or flowers that I heard. Let the context be your guide. Much of the information given here I was taught in previous encounters with the spirit forces in my life, so I was quite familiar with the material.

A simple note about the Guardians and the planes of manifestation is in order. The planes are energies in the invisible surround or ethers, which I felt and tracked as I moved through my own ascension process. On each level there are particular trials, certain ray colors, certain symbols and icons, and one overall quality of love that opened as I won through the trials. I could feel these as I steeped in each one for the two to six weeks it took to clear my way to the next level. There are 128 planes to pass through on the way to the Logos Sun, which I entered, with its fourteen concentric spheres. This Sun creates all forms in all worlds and all the experiences each form lives through. The Guardians are the twelve ray lords of the Logos spheres. They are bounded on the outside by Wisdom, the dark half of the Goddess, and at the center point by Unconditional Love or God/Goddess in their light forms, constantly creating within a loving partnership and union. It is their balanced and sovereign partnership that creates all forms and all flow within the cosmos. All of this is visually presented in the planes and Logos illustration at the end of chapter 2.

Well along in my personal process I began to feel that a single beloved had been created just for me and would come just for me. It was clear to me that this man would be for me alone a channel of love from the Christ or divine masculine within an intimate sacred sexual partnership, and I would be the same for him, bringing the Magdalene or divine feminine in Her light form. I could feel that while I had both inner male and female aspects in God/Goddess's image, I had left some part of myself behind. At birth, much of the male half of me was split off, forgotten, and lost to my awareness. This half is still near me, a closely attentive and deeply loving presence, though remaining in spirit form. It was this one who translated the answers of Christ/Magdalene into English and a consciousness format that I could understand. It was this one, too, who translated all the voices of the Guardians and the separate devas and djinns. In a way, then, we wrote this book together. He is in every way my love and the Christ/Magdalene's personal representative of love to and for me and no one else. He is the djinn who brings to me and into my field, spirit, soul, heart, mind, and body the Beloved stream of light from the Logos. He is my "higher self." I am told we all have a spirit beloved or half of self we left behind at birth, and one day the veil between us will disappear and we will be together again in bliss and sacred union forever, though in soul and spirit form only.

Until that time, we each have a human beloved, a person who has volunteered to serve the same function, to be God/Goddess's representative of intimate partnership and union with another in human form. This person is very like my spirit djinn partner. When beloveds come together in human form they truly are, for their partners, priest and priestess of the beloved stream from the Logos. This is a sacred and holy office and only one who has embodied wisdom can fill it. This is the Arthurian fulfillment and it is the blessing of the Christ/Magdalene for all who suffer through the wisdom climb. This passionate, mystical, and holy love in physical form is the highest blessing Heaven can bestow, and it will come to all who climb to the pinnacle. When you feel like giving up or not believing in love as the darkness tries to own you again, keep the promise of this blessing in your heart and hold onto it for all you are worth.

I have one last word, this one about the Mother. I have spent much of my life within a Christian tradition, Congregational and Presbyterian to be exact. The Mother is not mentioned in these traditions and Her Presence remains unknown. This is true for most traditions of the world. I simply wish to ask each of you who are skeptical about Her to set aside your disbelief for one twenty-four–hour period, just one day. Put it aside and agree to experience what comes and to let it change you. Ask Christ to lead and protect you, if you wish. Then, when this day is over, take back all your skepticism again, if you choose. I will tell you what happened to me when I did this. She came in silence and held me, held me with an intensity of love I hadn't experienced since before my biological mother died in 1981. I felt Her heartbeat next to mine. I felt pain being drawn from my belly to Hers, where it was remade into raw energy and sent back to revitalize me. I felt like a baby and I cried, for I had not known such gentle tenderness for so long. Then I watched Her merge into the Christ poster I have in my bedroom, a lovely image where He/She blends into the mountains and rivers of Earth. I saw Her Spirit enter His left Heart and become a shining light there, magnetic again, drawing us all Home to love. I saw Her Soul become hundreds of nature spirits pouring rainbow colors of love into every tree and flower and person on the planet. And I saw Her Body become the physical form of every living thing, the vessel that holds our souls and spirits through the journey we all take, humanity's long walk to divinity. (This is the human race, I think, and He/She is who we become at the finish line.) I could sense just how She feels all the emotional wounds in the nature spirits, for they are the creators of the emotional ethers and the emotional experiences of us all. I could sense how She feels all wounding to the feminine beloved in the Christ Heart within and *all physical pain of any kind in all forms across this planet.* I wept for all the times I have dishonored Her in my unknowing, perhaps most of all by being harsh with myself.

So, I have told this story and ask each person across this planet to feel Her, to soften the barriers between Her and your own self; for I believe that through this—and only through this—will come the salvation of the Earth. This and to help open and nourish the child hearts of all who read it are my two overriding reasons for transcribing this book.

May all who take in the words and emotions written or transcribed here be richly blessed. May wisdom dawn in every consciousness and heart across this lovely and loving planet. May the fulfillment come to each and every spirit, soul, heart, body, and mind. May all deep wounds of the Christ Heart be tenderly healed and the veil between worlds be melted in the loving hearts of humanity until they are no more and we can all be one family together again. And may the gentle and miraculous love of Christ/Magdalene enfold and nourish us, everyone, in each moment, now and forevermore. Praise be to God/Goddess!

§ 1 §

The Celtic Vows

There was a time before time when the waters of the cosmic sea were visible. One could sail to paradise and back and visit brothers and sisters in many worlds. Those days have passed for it was necessary to grow the great kingdom of humanity in separation from the consciousness of the All. But now humankind has grown to the level that the seas can once more be revealed, the pathways opened, and the human hearts that long for connection can be freed from their bondage. We, the Celts of old, the spirit forms in man, animal, tree, stone, fire, river, and sea have vowed to protect, guard and keep the Mother's Kingdom, to preserve its sanctity and gentle peace, which heals all pain and all memory of pain. We ache for your return. We have kept this vow: To maintain the isolated temples of stone, tree, river, and sea for tomorrow's children in deep respect and memory of the Living Mother Goddess. She is the One who holds All within Her womb of Love; recycling, renewing, rebirthing ever higher into the joy and greatness of Love. She of the deep mystery, invisible and invincible, carries us all through the circling moons, the circling suns, for the circle is Her form and indigo Her color. Know, child of the One, that whether you feel it or not, you are held each and every moment, now and forever, in Her arms of Love.

All who would follow the Celtic way and enter once again the great gateway into Her cosmic temple must take and keep Her vows. They are ancient and sacred. Misuse will be met with *instant* return of the same to the sender. The Mother's peace is inviolable, Her laws immutable, Her Love unsurpassable. Listen well.

THE CELTIC CODE

1. All honor is accorded to the Mother and Father, King and Queen of Heaven. Praise is free flowing, given daily and in joy, in any form desired by the adorer.

2. All forms of Her and His creation are honored and respected. All are recognized as equals, with their own powers of Love. Aside from the greatness of the Original Parents and the One Creator before them, no ranking is allowed.

3. All forms of life are regarded as temples and treated with gentle loving kindness at all times.

4. All worlds are visible, accessible, and interpenetrating, and work together to create new forms of love.

5. Thoughts, actions, and speech not based in love are not tolerated. Each form is responsible at all times for his/her actions, speech, and thoughts. Exceptions will create *instant* return to the sender as a gentle reminder that a boundary has been overstepped.

6. Mistakes are held in love, but continued and purposeful misuse will result in a probationary time and then the closing of the veil to allow the one who has not attained wisdom to continue his or her growth in one of the lower worlds.

7. There are inevitable tensions in growth. These will be addressed openly and collectively until a consensus is

reached. No communal action will take place until consensus has been achieved.

8. Rest (replenishment), work, service, and play in equal measure make for happiness.

9. The child, inner and outer, is allowed freedom to speak, grow, and create in equal balance with the inner and outer adult.

10. The male and female, inner and outer, are held as equal and their powers are used in balance and harmony.

11. The union of male and female is held as one of the most sacred forms of praise and worship.

12. The goal is creating in love, individually and together. All forces move toward higher and purer expressions of love.

13. All creating is done with conservation of energy and sustainability for all forms and in the spirit of fun and joy.

14. All planes are held as equal: the sensate, the emotional, and the mental levels, or sense, soul, and spirit. All levels are held in utmost respect, are treated with dignity, and are used to express and reveal love and love alone. None is considered above another.

15. The Christ, the Son of Man, is the guiding spirit of humanity and focalizes all radiations from the Mother and Father through His/Her Heart. These continuously create the evolution of humanity into His/Her likeness.

16. The Magdalene, His inner feminine nature, is recognized and honored for Her descent and for receiving and distributing His energies in the world of form, as well as for Her continued suffering in Love of the All.

17. The Iona, the Madonna, vessel of stone, protector of the child of light, is held in the utmost respect for Her great

strength, Her protection of the spirit child, Her descent, and Her Love.

18. The Father, who has alone held the higher worlds together, is honored for His strength, endurance, protection, and great Love.

19. Love of self is paramount, for it is recognized that all radiations of love stream from love of self. Self-disparagement and self-harm hold the highest priority for healing.

20. Sovereignty of all forms is law. No domination, no power struggle, no control, no force is ever tolerated at any level, spirit, soul, or sensate.

21. All mistakes are met with kindness and held in love and each is given a gentle reminder of the law. Punishment is forbidden.

22. Independence and intimacy are valued equally.

23. Peace is greatly valued—peace of spirit, soul, and sense. Any exceptions in song, dance, or worship are done with prior notice to and permission from all forms.

24. It is understood and accepted that the All is One Body and any disharmony in any world or at any plane affects the All. Exceptions are allowed only in the service of growth in love.

25. Patience is valued, for individual growth necessarily includes growth of the All. Personal will, timing, and desire are subdued in service to the All.

26. Simplicity is valued, both for its conservation of energy and its aesthetic of holding great love in minimal form.

27. Celebrations in tune with the astrological and planetary forces are held in every world and on all planes.

28. All participation is voluntary. Action, thought, or speech based in obligation is not tolerated.

29. The highest value at all levels and times is love. Actions, thoughts, and words created in purer and purer love are the primary goals.

30. Creation is the highest achievement. Invention and art, poetry, and song are highly valued as the bringing of the unrevealed into new forms of love.

31. The goals of society are healing and growth. All educators and healers are honored and supported.

32. There is a class whose members are guardians of the law and the purity of the Mother's Kingdom. These are the law givers and warriors. They are held in the highest esteem.

33. There is a class whose members are devoted to worship. These are the priests and priestesses, who are deeply honored and held in highest esteem by all levels of society.

34. The One Creator, Giver of All, Sustainer of All, fusion of Mother and Father, is adored and worshiped at all times and in every way.

35. Humor is held in the highest regard. All lessons, all experience, all life are taken with a grain of salt. There is dedication to humor.

36. Time is irrelevant. Rushing or hurrying is not allowed. Each unfolding or teaching is accepted as having its own natural timing of expression, and all are honored.

37. Experience is paramount. Lessons are learned and growth occurs primarily through experience and through play.

38. There is only Love. All forms on all planes make Love in all times and in all ways. There is service to Love and being in Love and Love alone, world without end.

INNER TRADITIONS

BEAR & CO.

HEALING ARTS PRESS

BEAR CUB BOOKS

DESTINY BOOKS

ParkStreet Press

BINDU BOOKS

Inner Traditions • Bear & Company

P.O. Box 388
Rochester, VT 05767-0388
U.S.A.

Affix
Postage
Stamp
Here

Please send us this card to receive our latest catalog.

☐ Check here if you would like to receive our catalog via e-mail.

E-mail address _____

Name _____ Company _____

Address _____

City _____ State _____ Zip _____ Country _____

Please check the following area(s) of interest to you:
☐ Health   ☐ Self-help   ☐ Science/Nature ☐ Shamanism
☐ Ancient Mysteries ☐ New Age/Spirituality ☐ Ethnobotany   ☐ Martial Arts
☐ Spanish Language   ☐ Sexuality/Tantra   ☐ Children   ☐ Teen

Order at 1-800-246-8648 • Fax (802) 767-3726
E-mail: orders@InnerTraditions.com • Web site: www.InnerTraditions.com

39. Death is seen for the illusion it is. There is continual change, recycling, and growth, but nothing is lost. All builds into higher forms and expressions of love.

40. Family is honored and supported, from the One Family to the nuclear family. Each is seen as a living organism and is respected and held in love.

41. Honesty and truth are paramount. Falseness, whether by omission or commission, is forbidden.

42. Purity is unrivaled in its essence. It is a goal to strive for at all times and in every endeavor. It is hoped for and embodied, but there is always room for growth.

These are the statutes of the law, the Chivalric Code of the Celtic Realm of Heaven. This world is at the Paradisiacal level and is the original source of all human descendants from the United Kingdom, the children of Ur. All who wish to enter herein must take the vow to uphold and honor the laws of the Mother/Father's Kingdom. So be it. Hurrah!

We of the spirit realms, those beyond the veil and those within the forms of animal, tree, plant, stone, water, and sky, honor all humanity for Her service to love, Her great suffering, and Her dedication to the development of individual consciousness and identity through the eons of separation, torture, and torment. Know that your great pain and your great and steadfast service to growth and goodness have been observed and honored on all planes and in all worlds. There are none who have suffered more. The esteem for humankind, for the great body of humanity at all levels knows no bounds. We are truly amazed at and reverent toward your ongoing dedication and great service to the All. The Mother wishes you to know that each one of the hue-men and women, at their attainment of wisdom and entrance into Her Kingdom, will be blessed beyond your current comprehension. You will walk among us as most highly revered teachers and saints. We are in awe at the great weight each of you has carried with strength, dignity, and responsibility to and beyond the breaking point. It is this capacity that brings you closest to the likeness of the One-In-All, and this is recognized and revered. Great joy and the greatest treasures of Love be yours, each and every one. You are so deeply and dearly loved!

THE GUARDIANS

2

The Invisible Structures of the Universe: The Great Heart Light Flowing to All Worlds

The Great Heart is the pump that pulses love into the cosmos. It does so using two beats in succession, just as the human heart does. The first beat is male; the second, a tiny bit stronger, is female. The first sends the light of love out of the Logos Sun, the second spreads it into all worlds. These pulses originate at the center point of the Logos Sun, and between beats the two Creators there, God and Goddess, come into a moment of full union and then partially separate again. Their suns merge for the smallest instant. The center point is like a perpetual orgasm and it does indeed create tiny photons that carry the message of love's ecstasy within them. These tiniest particles have yet to be discovered by the particle scientists, though this discovery is not far away. They are called the adamantine particles and are the building blocks of all else throughout the universe. Each particle contains all the qualities of God/Goddess in individualized form.

Adamantine particles are sent into the cosmos via the male radiatory force or electricity for the building of new varieties, forms, and revelations of love; for that is the sole purpose of all creation. They are sent in a precise direction with a specific destination in the Creators' Mind. The ray lords of the twelve fused Logos Suns—that is, the twelve concentric spheres all fused into one single Sun—blend these particles with various colors or rays. It should be noted that it is the *force of love* that is the basic essence of flow from the Creators into any and all specific forms. When the force of love is fused into a particular hue of light, this light takes on one of the qualities of love and is then called a ray. Such rays are formed by sending adamantine particles through very small geometric structures of light that then scatter and open the basic love qualities held within the structure.

There are twelve qualities, basic structures of God/Goddess, that are necessary for full divinity. The adamantine particles are not broken down by this process; they are simply infused strongly with one of these basic love qualities as they make their way through each layer of the Logos Sun so that the essence of this single quality shines more clearly than the rest for a time on each plane. But all twelve qualities of love are still contained in each and every particle.

Two other aspects of the Logos become activated by the center point of the Logos and the outermost plane. In the center point is the light of Christ/Magdalene (in Her light form), the quality of union, and this light is the central core of the heart of each human as well. The path to the embodiment of wisdom is implanted—via tiny light structures as the particles leave the Logos through the wisdom plane—by the Goddess in Her dark form, who will oversee growth in love's lessons of experience. These vary depending on the plane of existence to which the particle will descend. Those with the deepest descent have the longest and most difficult ascent as well.

The Pulse of the Creators is the cosmic heartbeat and its rhythm sets the pace for all life. Each time the Logos center unites and sends out a signal of love, all hearts in all beings in all worlds receive it and it revivifies them; the Christ/Magdalene light within each heart burns a tiny bit brighter for that instant. All hearts in all worlds are linked this way in the One Body of God/Goddess, and this is the mechanism for instant communication from one side of the universe to the other. It is not the strong nuclear force, nor the electrical, but another force yet to be discovered. This discovery will be the key to unlocking the unified field theory and many of the mysteries of the universe.

As the ray lords infuse the photons passing through twelve of the fourteen layers of the Logos Sun, the twelve basic aspects of divinity are activated and begin a process of unfoldment. Each and every particle has built within it the capability for full unfoldment into divinity. The tiny geometric structures that activate these basic divine qualities are overseen, or, as spirit would say, overlighted, by one ray lord, who is regent of that particular quality of love. These concentric ray spheres—the twelve fused Logos suns—are blended at the interface surface so there are no abrupt shifts from one to another.

We will explain the twelve ray-lord levels, as well as the ring just beyond the creator center point. The center point and Wisdom plane (the first plane) are not included in the numbering because the geometries of creation from these ray lords are built strictly on patterns of twelve.

The ray-lord level at the thirteenth Logos plane opens the four directions or the inner quadrants making up the structure of all forms in the universe, which begins the flow from the creator center point outward. This ray lord's physical creation on Earth is the insect kingdom, which is made up of hidden winged forces in service to the four streams of the creator flow of God/Goddess.

The ray of the twelfth Logos plane infuses the particles with personal passion for God/Goddess or the Beloved aspect of the Creators, who are first and foremost the source of all love for any individual. This is the level at which the genders of each individual being are activated. Each individual male is fused in pure union with and love of the Goddess, and each female with God, so a beloved union with the individual's opposite gender of God/Goddess is anchored into place. This makes God/Goddess the true love partner for all forms.

From the ray of the eleventh Logos plane comes the formation, for each being, of a single personal partner of the same fully unfolded form so that each unfolded being has a personal beloved in their own form. This duality opens the qualities of true love, adoration, and desire. Each partner is essentially a priest or priestess of the Beloved stream from God/Goddess for their one partner in form.

At the tenth Logos plane the entire drama of love is put into place and the level of descent and length of the cycle of return are chosen. Very specific icons and memories are put into place or encoded in the individual. These are carefully opened after the descent to create the outer experiences that will draw the individual through their path of ascent and back to union with God/Goddess.

In the ninth Logos plane, the rays bring about the expansion of the inner light into mind, heart, and body. Three inner suns form within each particle, and each aspect unfolds according to the separate waves or timing. Human beings are a precise replica of the Logos Sun. They, too, create adamantine particles in the three creator lights located in the deep heart, mind, and base. In the Logos these three lights are fused into one, but in the human they are separated, creating the intellectual, emotional, and physical experiences of a person in direct connection with and surrender to the will of the One Logos Sun. The creator force of the heart is exactly double that of each of the other two; in this way, balance is achieved.

To ease confusion, let us explain the waves of creation emanating from the Logos Sun as they affect the Earth. These are pulses of light and love streaming down from the Logos through the 128 spirit, soul, and sensate realms. This will help to unravel confusions surrounding the ancient stoneworks of your planet. The wave of emotional experiences is on a twenty-four–day, or two-times-twelve–day lunar cycle. The female and male aspects of each ray lordship take one day each per lunar month and there are fifteen lunar months in a single solar year. Five intercessory days, November 23–November 27, are not considered a moon because the geometries of the subtle structures in all forms built by this wave are built strictly on the number fifteen. The Mother is sole regent of this wave.

The wave of intellectual growth is on a thirty-day or three-times-ten–day lunar cycle, with twelve moons in the solar year. Again, there are five intercessory days, December 18–December 22, just prior to midwinter, and, again, these are not counted as a moon because the geometries are built strictly on a pattern of twelve. The Father is sole regent of intellectual growth.

The wave of physical experiences is on a twenty-eight–day or four-times-seven–day lunar cycle. There are thirteen moons in one solar year and one intercessory day, December 25. The fused boy/girl androgyne is sole regent of physical manifestation.

The five inner planes of the Logos (the tenth Logos plane through the fourteenth Logos plane) make up the mystical path, a one-to-one love relationship between God/Goddess and the individual. This path always unfolds in a completely individualized fashion and does not lend itself to organized structure of any kind. The emphasis is not on the outer world, but on the unseen and the emotion felt within each individual and God/Goddess. The creations on Earth of the five Logos planes, ten through fourteen, are flowers. Every flower, in both form and scent, is linked to a love memory experienced at these four levels before the descent, and flowers can and do open these memories and feelings quite powerfully.

On the eighth Logos plane, the realm of the Father, the light is made visible. Light is sent into these previously hidden structures and they begin to glow. The quality of love infused on this plane is glory and the outer world is then created by the visualizations, emotions, and actions of the three inner creator lights—mind, heart, and body—in each particle. Each creator light makes its own outer reality, which in turn reflects its inner light. This is true for all forms. All planes from here on create outer realities that can be seen, a blend or shared collective reality of each individual's inner light.

The seventh Logos plane is the Mother, consort of the Father. She creates the outer vessel or container in which the three creator lights of mind, heart, and body grow. This vessel provides a specific body for each individual to live and act within and is precisely determined by the plane of descent to which each is going. The goddess Liberty is regent of this plane.

The sixth Logos plane is the Arthurian realm, where the family or clan is put into place. The true love partners live within a specific society and family structure here, which prepares them for the world they will descend to and their unfoldment. Each family has a certain commitment to God/Goddess, a stewardship of certain aspects of the world of form they will go to, and a responsibility to serve as a group in caring for specific aspects of creation in that world. The fifth ray plane is the little girl or virgin aspect. A separate light different from the creator sun is created in the heart of each individual. This separate and new light is a sanctuary of deep and holy communion between the individual and the opposite gender aspect of God/Goddess, linking that individual with his or her Beloved in the center point of the Logos. It is a place deep in the heart where each can sense the One, a place of solace for all beings entering into worlds of fear. It is this place where partnership with God/Goddess is felt, where specific questions can be asked and answers given, and where plans and dreams can be made together. The little girl aspect then creates the combined heart's desires of the One and herself into the physical realm.

The fourth ray-lord plane is the little boy aspect. He is the magician, the one who creates connections with others in the physical realm. He is in full union with the little girl aspect; they, in fact, create their outer reality together within a sacred sexual partnership. But he is also keeper of the personal will, the inner dragon, and must learn to balance his own needs and directions with those of God/Goddess and to balance his own needs with those for the greater good.

The third Logos plane is the Mother, who is water. She is the river of life and Her life-giving waters begin the flow of emotional experience with a cyclical forward flow that is felt as time. She is the wave of universal, ongoing emotional unfoldment; she sets timing and a personal deep-heart connection into each individual and then coordinates all forms in one grand symphony of unfoldment. It is Her force that provides the forward movement of all life and development. Mother Mary is regent here.

The second Logos plane is the Elohim, twelve huge suns that circle the Logos and infuse each individual with one grand purpose or mission to reveal their own divinity and the great love of God/Goddess. This is the destiny stream and it leads all into full unfoldment of their divinity.

The physical expression on Earth for the first through the fourth Logos planes is the mineral kingdom. The first or outermost Logos plane is the Wisdom path, the lessons of love embodied in the heart. This can only be renewed by a full and painful separation from the awareness of love and God/Goddess and then the relearning of love's lessons in a painful climb, where the personal will is broken down and darkness within is transmuted by the individual pushing with all his or her might against the non-love forces. This is the unseen or dark aspect of the Goddess. It holds all vibrations of non-love, which are, in truth, love taught by experience, so they are fully embodied into the emotional system and can be lived as naturally as breathing. The goddess Iona is overlighting regent of this emotional path of experience and the embodiment of wisdom by all humans. She is The One who descended with us to bear all pain, and it is She who walks beside each disciple as their consciousness ascends, until the five inner planes of the Logos are reached. Then the Goddess Magdalene takes over this function of the divine feminine, reawakening a personal relationship with each individual.

Humanity has a full commitment to renew two of the Logos levels, the unconditional love of the center point and the Wisdom stream. The white of unconditional love blended with the indigo of wisdom is the cobalt ray color of Earth and is the central ray aspect of all human beings. There are no worlds with more suffering or more darkness to face and clear than Earth, and what is endured on Earth is beyond the imagining of those in spirit and soul planes. We honor you, everyone who carries so much that the love and wisdom streams

may be renewed, for the One is a living God/Goddess and these qualities of love and wisdom can be revitalized only by being lived. Earth
is the breeding ground of all spiritual warriors, and all who come to
Earth have unsurpassed courage and devotion to God/Goddess. This
is recognized and honored by all beings in all worlds. To you is given
the magical fulfillment *in the physical.* This highest of blessings is
awarded only to those who suffer the full descent and ascent, taking
on all the wounds of darkness and facing and transmuting these in
love. All beings in all realms kneel before you of humanity in admira-
tion, respect, and abiding love. Take this in for just a moment and feel
it for it is pure and radiant truth.

All twelve ray lords serve God/Goddess in both Her dark and
light forms. And three more overlighting ray lords oversee the twelve
Logos planes, except the center point and Wisdom levels, which are
directed by God/Goddess alone.

Thus, the adamantine particles are made into a refined light with
the pure and intense rainbow colors of the Logos Sun. This Logos
light is the DNA or the strong nuclear force that holds the patterns of
unfoldment for that individual who will eventually affect the All. That
is, these levels of unfoldment will ripple out to touch all beings in all
worlds and change them toward higher expressions of love. Seven of
these colors can be seen in the outer world; five cannot be seen. The
three overlighting ray lords oversee the Logos light going to the
twelve chakras of all individuals. The chakras are inner ray keepers or
centers of each individual being that match precisely the structure of
the Logos itself. The angelic kingdom serves the twelve ray lords and
God/Goddess or the Logos Sun directly.

Each plane in the Logos and on the spirit, soul, and sensate levels
carries one quality or force of love down, through, and out of the
Logos and spreads it to all forms in all worlds in the form of rays of
light. There is one overlighting being at each level who is in service
to the Logos and is responsible for all teachings at that level.

Descending out of the Logos are the sixty-six planes of the spirit
realms, where spirit forms live. The creation of the spirit realms on

Earth is the plant kingdom, with the exception of flowers. The planes of the spirit realms are overseen by three spirit ray lords, djinn forces who oversee the radiation of all electrical streams of the Father as it affects all worlds. These djinns are masculine in nature and are skilled in bringing light into the mind. Powerful winged beings, they create all intellectual and spiritual growth and unfoldment in the inner planes and outer worlds and bring light into most plants and insects. This light contains certain structured encoded messages that jump start the electrical or intellectual growth of each being. Djinns are made of light, but it is not adamantine in nature; it is constructed of geometric forces similar to the protein structures of the human body. Djinn forces are in the service of the male Creator or Christ.

Below or surrounding the spirit realms are the forty-four planes of the soul realms overseen by three soul ray lords. The creations of the soul realms in the outer world on Earth are animals. The soul realms are made of a watery or liquid light substance created from the Logoic DNA, the electrical spirit radiation, and the magnetic souls force, along with precise geometric inner structures formed by the Logos and/or soul ray lords. Water is a unique substance—it holds the structures of emotion, carries the flow of feeling, and is susceptible to great change as it reflects or takes on the characteristics of all emotional flow. The soul realms hold every quality of love and its polar opposite. These realms are overseen by the Mother Magdalene, who is regent over all emotional experiences of all beings in accordance with the grand plan of the Creators and in alignment with the intellectual flow of the Father. She is served by the devic kingdom, primarily feminine soul beings or devas who bring these watery energies into all forms.

Finally, three physical ray lords serving the Magdelene oversee the eighteen physical planes. The creation of these planes is humanity, and they are served by all forces, angelic, djinn, and devic in their full unfoldment into personal, expressed divinity, the Arthurian fulfillment, and reunion with God/Goddess. These planes are the expression of the little girl and little boy aspects, the Holy Spirit, and the personal will in connection with the All. They are co-creators in part-nership with God/Goddess. All humans will one day learn to mani-fest their heart's desires into the physical (in full alignment with the will of the Creators and the timing of the Father and Mother). Humans are all magicians in training and will in time perform won-ders of physical manifestation.

Each individual creation of these realms, whether flower, mineral, plant, or animal, brings specific and precise messages from the planes to which their consciousness is linked, and all are happy to serve. In another book it would be useful to describe the differences in con-sciousness of spirit, soul, and physical life forms, for they are quite marked. Flowers, for instance, have none of the guardedness of humans and are much like infants; they severely feel damage done to them. But they are healed nearly instantly by the miraculous Logos forces to which they are intimately connected. Yet, because God/Goddess feel everything, it would be best if this wounding did not occur.

The descriptions in the following chapters of this book are pre-cisely ordered to fit the overall heart structure of the universe and, when read, will open and activate precise levels of the reader's deep heart, which is the Divine Child within, the Holy Spirit of the little girl and boy who hold the full memories of these ancient planes, the truth of love, and the eternal prior to the descent into darkness. It is the work of the spirit world to help all reach their divinity, and all in spirit hope for this as soon as it may be.

A person's complete unfoldment is seeded into his or her deep heart, spinal, and reproductive structures. Rapid ascension for those on Earth is now possible. Our scribe began at the lowest levels and has progressed to the innermost planes of the Logos in five and a half years of steady clearing meditations, each one to two hours per day. Her consciousness was very structured in the personality distortions (the severely consciousness-limiting result of having taken in down to the sensate level the illusions of all planes) because it had lived within them for many, many years—nearly thirty—before she began her ascension process. Hers has been an intensive climb and this level of speed is not recommended for everyone. We simply point out that it is possible to go from severely distorted levels and lives bounded by fear to great heights and magical co-creation with God/Goddess in a very short amount of time. It is the wish of all in spirit form to see that every person who is suffering within a consciousness of fear finds a clearing method and begins the work of clearing. There are great changes in store for the Earth plane and these changes will demand an enlightened consciousness for all who wish to remain here and be sustained at the physical level. The Arthurian fulfillment will become a living reality for many in a very short time. This means that pure co-creative partnerships with God/Goddess will be achieved and create new and startling changes in this physical reality. These changes will bring about great peace and stability within a love consciousness here, but they will be upsetting, even disturbing, to a consciousness still locked in fear. It will become more and more difficult to live here and hold onto the old fear-based belief structures; the mental expansion required will be nearly impossible to achieve and so we wish to urge all who have not begun inner clearing work to do so with all speed.

The Arthurian fulfillment and the ability to manifest or co-create in the physical with God/Goddess as personal partner have been decreed since the beginning of creation. The millennium shift allows the final push into full unfoldment of the human-divine creations—very much like the Master, Jesus Christ—that every human is meant to become. The way to unfoldment is steep and painful because all fears must be faced and transmuted in love. But to any who realize that the outer world is a figment of the collective imagination and consciousness, these frightening occurrences will be taken for what they are, non-truths that can be cleared out of one's system simply and gradually, and then never faced again. Those who experience these outer occurrences as real and as having power to create permanent damage will have a much more difficult time. Please try to realize that the outer world is just the human collective consciousness at work, nothing more.

We do understand there is great suffering occurring on your planet at this time. Every being at every level feels this, too, for the cosmic consciousness is One consciousness, even if all in spirit form do not experience physical pain. Yet it would help greatly for all to realize and hold this truth: Every event coming into your lives is created by you; all spirit and soul forces are in pure service of humanity's evolution and divinity and create these outer events simply to bring to each person's attention the fears carried within that need to be healed. Not one thing is intended to cause harm. And when one makes a commitment to clear all fear and then sticks to this commitment religiously, the spirit forces will go to great lengths to bring fear reflections as gently as possible—such as in newspaper articles or novels. No one could suffer all wounds of the descent and survive.

We feel there are a few more important things to say here. There are many who begin to feel their divinity, to understand they are truly children of God/Goddess and have divine powers, and this is truth. But though they feel this, they may not yet have cleared their personal power or will distortions and blended fully with the Will force of the Logos. They may think they can magically escape the difficulties of transformation and the painful wisdom lessons, or they may believe they can save the world with a wave of the hand. These are fanatical streams and are as in need of clearing as all other distortions. They are never truth and we wish to alert you to their existence simply to save you from these dangerous streams that can be very tempting to those in emotional pain. Change is made gradually *within*—then, *and only then,* will the outer dramas or reflections improve.

Quite simply, the ascension process breaks down the entire structure of the personality, soul, and spirit that is based in fear. This fear is old and deep and has been lived out in many lives. Breaking down the personal will—in particular, the inner dragon—is a difficult and painful process and requires strong faith and strong hearts. For the heart to deepen into an acceptance of all suffering and acceptance in the heart of all who undergo it, it must be broken over and over again.

This deepening is the essence of the wisdom climb and will produce a fully opened and compassionate heart.

The days are fast approaching when this climb will be mandatory for everyone on Earth. It is time for Heaven to appear, to manifest in the physical. This is the will of God/Goddess. As the creator force intensifies here with the ascension of many to the level of creator-hood, center point of the Logos, the collective thoughts, emotions, and actions of all will manifest quite powerfully in outer experiences. It will be best to have cleared any and all thoughts and inner forces that wish to create harm to another. And because of the law of return—"One gets what one gives"—the one who wishes ill to someone will draw back on himself or herself that same force for harm. On the other hand, miracles will become daily events and those who wish for world peace will get it. The time for full magic and creatorhood to become a reality is very close.

There are many who say that the arrival of these days will mean the annihilation of the world and much of humanity. This is simply not truth, for all will be given a choice. Each and every person will be called to find a spiritual path and begin this passage of clearing fear and embodying wisdom in preparation for the opening of the creator powers. At first, the call will be gentle. But as the time grows short and difficulties in consciousness become more intense, so will the messages from the spirit realm become stronger, perhaps uncomfortably so, especially if a person does not respond to calls given in any other way. The patterns holding a person back from true happiness will be activated and will become more and more apparent in their lives. If a person does not recognize this discomfort as a message from the spirit world and so begin an inner healing path, the pain could become quite intense—we will go to great lengths to try to reach *everyone*. We wish for true and lasting joy for every single person on Earth. Any pain that is felt does not mean the spirit world wishes to harm anyone; quite the contrary—we are committed to and in full service of helping to free humanity from fear so the happily ever after can begin. It is because these changes are necessary to avoid fragmentation of consciousness in the near future that we try so hard to reach you.

So when the call comes from us, we urge you to begin. Choose whatever spiritual tradition is most comfortable for you and a spiritual friend you can call on for emotional support or shoring up of faith when difficulties arise, as they inevitably will. These difficulties will reflect each individual's inner fears quite precisely, fears that have built up over many, many lives and are held in the deep unconscious. There are very few who have opened their minds to the level of recalling past lifetimes, and it is not at all necessary to do so. Spirit will gradually and surely lead any and all who are committed. There is no need to be concerned. The wisdom climb is simply a process of growth, self-empowerment, standing in love no matter what, and developing or remembering the love-based consciousness and beliefs that are everyone's deepest truth. We simply help you to clean the jewels that you truly are underneath, to reflect purely and miraculously the love of God/Goddess. Keep to your practice of clearing. Do not give in or give up, no matter what happens, and you will be lead safely and surely through the narrows.

We have two final comments: First, it is not possible to avoid emotional pain; all are meant to be tested to see if they will hold to love in the face of great darkness. Those who do not hold to love will not be admitted to Heaven *in the physical realm* when it arrives, and that time is fast approaching. The winnowing process has begun. This process is simply one of selecting individuals who are willing to brave the deepest darkness in the service of love, to answer love's call when God/Goddess make requests. Sometimes requests for service come with little or no notice. Sometimes the risk and energy demanded are great. But this is what is needed to secure the highest forces of light in a realm where darkness has ruled for centuries. And Heaven in the physical realm is a gift of great value, given by God/Goddess in gratitude to the spiritual warriors for love who serve during these troubled times of transformation from darkness to light—that is all. No one is better than another; such competitive thinking is utterly false. All are greatly valued and loved for whatever they choose to give in service to love's call.

Second, what will become of those who do not make it? Some have already chosen to take their lives or have succumbed to illness or other fragmenting forces—they will simply go to Heaven on the other side of the veil. They will enter the soul or spirit realms, serve the evolution of the All in soul or spirit form, and will be with their beloved at that level. This simply means they will not experience the Arthurian fulfillment *in the physical*. At soul and spirit levels this fulfillment has always been the only way; they will simply go to Heaven.

There may be some who feel that it is best to leave this world of suffering and return to soul or spirit form. But we emphasize that being in physical form is an exquisite thing. For we of spirit do not feel the wind on our faces or the touch of a friend. We do feel emotion and spirit exchanges, but that is all. Experiencing a sacred sexual union in the physical and being able to manifest your personal and planetary heart's desires *in the physical,* in the *exact image* of God/Goddess, is a truly miraculous experience. There are thousands of spirits who would have chosen to do this, but only the most courageous were allowed. Therefore, ponder your choices before you make them and choose carefully.

We wish all well on their chosen journeys to full creatorhood. May rich pleasure, surprise, and abundant wisdom reach to the depths of each heart, and may every single person on Earth feel often along the way the true and lasting joy and full and loving embrace of God/Goddess. Be blessed and loved, each and every one.

YOUR BROTHERS AND SISTERS OF THE SPIRIT WORLD,
THE GUARDIANS, RAY LORDS, ANGELS, DEVAS AND DJINNS,
FLOWERS, MINERALS, PLANTS, AND ANIMALS

Fig. 2.1. The 128 Planes of Form, with the Rays of Logos stepped down through all planes.

Descending: Planes of descent and human development, conception to midlife. Ascending: Planes of ascent and human development, midlife to death. *Please note*: Items with asterisks (*) signify the Five Pillars of Divinity.

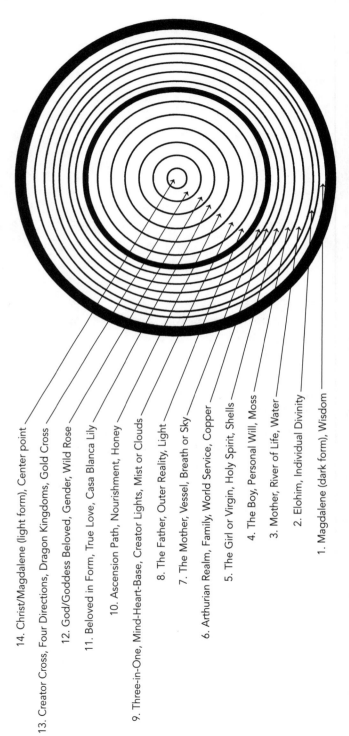

THE LOGOS

14. Christ/Magdalene (light form), Center point

13. Creator Cross, Four Directions, Dragon Kingdoms, Gold Cross

12. God/Goddess Beloved, Gender, Wild Rose

11. Beloved in Form, True Love, Casa Blanca Lily

10. Ascension Path, Nourishment, Honey

9. Three-in-One, Mind-Heart-Base, Creator Lights, Mist or Clouds

8. The Father, Outer Reality, Light

7. The Mother, Vessel, Breath or Sky

6. Arthurian Realm, Family, World Service, Copper

5. The Girl or Virgin, Holy Spirit, Shells

4. The Boy, Personal Will, Moss

3. Mother, River of Life, Water

2. Elohim, Individual Divinity

1. Magdalene (dark form), Wisdom

Spirit Levels
Star Family
128. Birthday Cake: Birth of star child
127. Daffodil Sun: Star family holding hands in a circle
126. Dragonfly Woods: Boy becomes nature spirit, girl becomes inner essence
125. Dragonfly Sun: Boy covers girl to keep her safe
124. Cosmic Ocean: Mother enfolds Divine Child in salt water
123. Baptismal River: Mother baptizes Divine Child with fresh water

Divine Mother/Child Descent
122. Apple Orchard: Eternal day; Mother, Father, and child together
121. Rainbow Sun: Mother, Father, and child choose colors for child's star
120. The Abyss: Mother descends into darkness and realms ruled by god of fear; split into good and bad halves
119. Child Jesus Carrying Lamb: Divine Boy agrees to be Lamb of God, to be sacrificed; descends into realm ruled by god of darkness
118. Skeleton: Divine Child recedes inside crystals in bones
117. Armor: Divine Child puts on bony covering

Divine Androgyne Spirit
116. Cross: Divine heart split into four pieces— Mother, Father, Girl, Boy
115. Earth Butterfly: Divine Girl prepares to descend to Earth; cloaks her light in darkness
114. Closed Doors: Memory of Heaven closed into deep unconscious
113. Shepherd Boy: Divine Child disguised as poor shepherd boy
112. Slavery: Divine Child taken into slavery by overlord of fear
111. Bedrock: Divine Child hides magic powers in testicles to stay safe

Divine Boy Sprit
110. Sinew: Divine Boy tied to the mast through the storm
109. Auric Egg: Divine Boy enclosed in bubble, alone, in separation from the One
108. Ribs: Divine Boy puts on breastplate of a warrior; agrees to hunt and be hunted
107. Baby in Basket in the River: Divine Boy chooses a spiritual destiny
106. Trout: Divine Mother encloses spiritual destiny in still-small pool in Divine Boy's heart
105. Salmon: Divine Boy agrees to upstream struggle to return to Mother for rebirth

Divine Girl Spirit
104. Exile: Divine Child leaves Mother and Homeland; agrees to work for love
103. Little Black Girl, Smile: Divine Girl splits from Divine Boy; disguised as dark child, agrees to bear his wounds
102. Peasant Woman: Divine Mother (aspect of Divine Girl) disguised as peasant to care for neglected children
101. Puppy Dog: Divine Girl sends her heart love into skin, loving through touch

100. Tears: Divine Girl sends her heart love into tears, loving through empathy

99. Curly Baby Hair: Divine Girl sends her heart love into hair, brings thoughts of love into world

Divine Mother Spirit

98. Abdomen, Ocean: Divine Mother carries all unconscious wounds of Divine Children that wait for healing

97. Shepherdess: Divine Mother disguised as teacher to guide Divine Children to their Home

96. Rivers: Divine Mother disguised as fresh water to cleanse and ease children's thirst for love

95. Madonna: Divine Mother disguised as nun to care for neglected spirits of Divine Children

94. Fabrics: Divine Mother disguised as sheets, clothes, towels, blankets to hold Her children

93. Motherhood: Divine Mother disguised as human mother to love each child intimately

92. Cream: Divine Mother disguised as cream and butter to nourish Divine Children

91. Skin: Divine Mother disguised as skin to hold her children

90. Mother's Milk: Divine Mother disguised as breast milk to nourish her children

Divine Father Spirit

89. Ark of the Covenant: Divine Father agrees to care for all kingdoms on Earth

88. Fisherman: Divine Father disguised as fisherman to lead child to his or her destiny

87. River Mouth: Divine Father agrees to lead child back to the One Mother

86. Father Fishing with Child: Divine Father agrees to guide child to hidden wisdom

85. Long Grasses: Divine Father agrees to farm and work, to feed and care for child

84. Fatherhood: Divine Father agrees to be human father to love each child personally

83. Oyster: Divine Father holds Holy Books and memory of pearls of Truth

82. Tidal Mudflats: Father keeps memories of ancient life

81. Marsh Grass/Crew Cut: Father helps bring ancient knowledge into practical use

Grandfather Spirit

80. Carpenter: Grandfather helps build child's form

79. Tree Man: Grandfather brings streams of knowledge into books

78. Seaweed: Grandfather is magic dragon, electricity to help child create better

77. The Oil Man: Grandfather breaks down old life into oil or raw energy for child

76. Peat: Grandfather stores ancient memories in the unconscious

75. Stone, Miner: Grandfather stores precious jewels of wisdom within hard work of seeking

74. Fire: Grandfather stokes fire of passion to fuel work

73. Lava: Grandfather brings ancient hidden passions to surface

72. Sea Captain: Grandfather puts child on his or her ship of destiny

Grandmother Spirit

71. Snow, Starlight: Grandmother sends dreams to star child

70. Fairy Godmother: Grandmother helps child create with imagination

69. Meadows: Grandmother disguised as meadows to nourish freedom of child spirit

68. Herb Woman: Grandmother disguised as herbs and medicine woman to heal child

67. Gingerbread: Grandmother disguised as grains, bread, and cookies to nourish child

66. Grandmother: Grandmother disguised as simple home in the forest to hold child

65. Dolmens: Grandmother in sacred, wet, rocky sites to rebirth Divine Child

64. Lichens/Snakes: Grandmother disguised as powerful transformations

63. Moss: Grandmother leads the child Home along ancient path

SOUL LEVELS

62. Lily: Girl becomes essence of true love

61. Unicorn: Boy and girl separate; girl becomes fairy spirit, boy becomes pixie or gnome spirit

Soul Girl

60. Fern: Girl keeps memory of stairway to Heaven

59. Cave: Girl becomes womb, breaks down the old and rebirths the new

58. Cave Opening: Girl becomes birth canal for child

57. Dromenon: Girl holds the blueprint for path of experience in child's life

56. Gong: Girl becomes the call to new life

55. Temple Door: Girl leads child to inner temple

54. Burning Bush: Girl becomes fire to purify the spirit

Soul Boy

53. Rabbit: Boy is bridge to nature spirits, shaman

52. White Crane: Boy journeys into spirit world for new knowledge

51. Otter: Boy makes inner connections to friends in spirit world, cosmic ocean of the Mother

50. White Dog: Boy is great heart of the animal kingdom, best friend of child

49. Storms, Lightning: Boy releases and balances conflict in child by angry outbursts

48. White Lion, Storms: Boy guards and fiercely protects divine heart of the child

47. Stag/Dusk: Boy disguised as animals and forest to give peace to child spirit

Girl/Boy Soul

46. Cherry Tree: Girl and Boy loves meet each other

45. Silver Wheel: Blending of love of masculine and feminine

44. Tulips: Passion of first love

43. Communion: Blending of spirits of masculine and feminine

42. Checkerboard: Blending different identities of each other in play

41. Soccer Ball: Blending each other's inner child in play

40. Tribe around Campfire: Family together in darkness

Soul Families

39. Drumming Circle: Dancing together to beat of life
38. Hippo: Touching, being together in communal family
37. Papyrus: Communicating with each other, speech
36. Black Mother and Father: Agree to care in hearth and home for all children in darkness
35. Raccoon: Boy longs to return to True Mother, spirit world
34. Salmon: Boy decides to go back Home for rebirth
33. Brown Bear: Boy goes to forest or natural world to seek True Mother; rape of Boy; closing of Boy Spirit

Soul Mother

32. Grizzly Bear: True Mother protects child and naturalness of spirit
31. Triple Horse: True Mother nurtures freedom of spirit, mother, father, child
30. Dust Storms: True Mother creates whirlwind to free child spirit
29. Elephant: True Mother teaches how to bring spirit into action in service
28. Eucalyptus: True Mother teaches how to bring spirit into breath
27. Wolf: True Mother brings connection to spirit world through nature
26. Tarapin*: True Mother teaches patient endurance through pain of rebirth

Soul Father

25. Bull*: True Father teaches how to carry heavy burdens of humanity
24. Gold Lion*: True Father teaches courage in facing great fear
23. Sphinx: True Father teaches sacred mysteries from the spirit world before the flood
22. Joan of Arc*: Girl aligned with True Father, teaches how beliefs create outer reality
21. King Arthur*: True Father makes commitment to become world server
20. Ash Tree: True Father supports creativity of the spirit child
19. Mango: First sexual union

SENSATE LEVELS

Solar Father

18. The Sun: True Father teaches how to love whole world
17. Mint: True Father teaches cleansing of speech

Lunar Mother

16. The Moon: True Mother teaches how to love intimately
15. Mother's Milk: True Mother nourishes child with self love

Star Child

14. Homestar: Jesus, True Child, helps build specific personality for child to help all humanity
13. Michael Forces: Light forces teach child to use love to transform darkness

PERSONALITY LEVELS

12. Mickey Mouse: Spirit world teaches boy to create through imagination
11. Jesse: True Mother brings unlimited possibilities for child to create
10. Abraham: True Father teaches tasks that will free children from their slavery to fear
9. Oceanna: True Mother teaches how to hold everyone in harmony
8. Star of Bethlehem: Girl holds Divine Child in her womb

Rape of the Girl, Closing of the Soul

7. Sophia: True Girl teaches going into deep unconscious of humanity to transform fear
6. Ganesh: True Father teaches focus and determination to clear obstacles
5. Higher Self: Spirit half that was left behind at birth, the spirit partner
4. Merlin: Spirit teachers that teach ways to transform the spirit
3. King Arthur: Commitment to unify self, soul, and spirit for good of all
2. The New Jerusalem: Commitment to unite inner divine heart for good of all
1. Central Sun: Commitment to unite inner masculine and feminine for good of all

ENTRANCE INTO THE PHYSICAL REALM
SPLITTING OF MASCULINE AND FEMININE INTO TWO STREAMS

MASCULINE PATHWAY

Sirius A: True father teaches responsibility for ourselves in the world outside the home.

Polaris: True masculine holds us to the central axis of pure love, male beloved.

Mars: True boy teaches us to be a spiritual warrior in the physical world.

The Sun: True masculine teaches us to give all love openly to the whole world in love.

Human Vessel: Masculine stream enters the crown and descends through the spine as the clockwise half of the creator helix.

FEMININE PATHWAY

Sirius B: True mother teaches responsibility for ourselves in the home and family.

The Moon: True feminine teaches us to receive all and transform it in love, feminine beloved.

Venus: True girl teaches us to share the wounds of humanity in love.

Earth: True feminine teaches us how to take care of physical needs in love.

Human Vessel: Feminine stream enters the base and ascends through the spine as the counterclockwise creator.

3

The Tree Kingdom:
Wisdom Keepers

We of the tree kingdom are joyful at the opportunity to speak at last.
We are thankful to the mind that listens and translates our thoughts
for humanity to hear and understand.

The first thing we must say is this: Though these chapters are
grouped by the great kingdoms in the Earth Mother's world of form,
all such divisions are never hard and fast. We are all interrelated and work
together in service to the One, to Love. But each kingdom or group
consciousness has its own purpose, its own forward focus or mission.

We of the tree kingdom are the great keepers of wisdom. It is
important to state that wisdom is not the same as knowledge, and,
while we are actively involved in the distribution of knowledge
through our contribution to the making of books and paper, our
highest aim is to help humanity attain their level and lessons of wisdom. We are directed by the dark half of the Goddess—whom some
call Sophia—who also directs the wisdom rays from the Logos, while
the Iona descends to walk with each disciple as they climb. We bring
the energies of these lessons of experience through our etheric chan-

nels into our heartwood, and, from there, breathe them out into the air that surrounds you. Even the wood in your home is still breathing, though at a slower rate.

The intuitions you have are a direct result of our work in the world. The trees surrounding your place of living or work, the wood you choose for your furniture can tell you a great deal about the teachings you are being given at this time in your life. These trees and this wood are your current teachers of the lessons of the heart, chosen specifically for you by the Christ to bring you Home. Often changes of location are created for a person simply to bring his or her soul closer to the necessary tree teachers.

Our purpose is to bring all of humankind into the wisdom levels through experiential learning of the painful lessons of life. We hold the peace of those lessons. We flood you at all times with the highest understandings related to the pain and confusion you are undergoing. We are great healers of the heart and emotional pain, and the variety of substances or essences made from us could bring about tremendous healing of heart ailments of all kinds. We would ask someone who's interest in such healing is passionate to work with us in bringing this information to light, for it could be done in a very short time. When all of humanity has attained its wisdom status, there will be a period of rest and play. Then a new purpose for all kingdoms will be chosen. That time grows near and we are collectively holding these possibilities in our consciousness now.

There are classes of trees as there are races of humanity. Each has specific wisdom teachings and dedication to individual purposes. In general, within these divisions by purpose the varieties are deciduous, evergreen, and succulent. Within these three categories are divisions related to the physical gifts we create and offer to humanity. These are fruit, wood, leaf, bark, and root. There are also divisions based on the veining pattern of our leaves. All forms are color coded; bark brown and leaf green will tell you that our purpose involves the heart, for both of these rays are found within the heart grid.

Because the purpose of this book is the explanation of the Celtic path of ascension, which we support, we will give simply a brief description of the purposes of these divisions and leave a fuller account for another time.

DIVISIONS BY PURPOSE

Deciduous

The deciduous trees are dedicated to working within the lunar/ solar cycle of gestation. Their teachings follow this cycle closely, so that summer transmissions are more concerned with relationships in the outer world and winter transmissions are more concerned with a person's inner world. Spring and fall relate respectively to the growth of new talents or tasks and then the breakdown of these in preparation for the recycling process of winter. All of these transmissions are attuned quite specifically to the person or people near whom they live.

Evergreen

The conifers, or evergreens, are dedicated to bringing, through the memories and the development of the highest standards of eternal love, the everlasting truths, those laws that do not change or pass away. There is an uplifting quality to the great conifers, such as the redwoods, that cannot be found with the same degree of intensity at any other place in the Earth realm. They are the temples, the sanctuaries of this planet, and they hold this dedication in the face of severe destruction. They are particularly helped in their purposes by the owls, who work closely with them. Evergreen messages are not so individualized, for the highest standards these great trees hold are meant for all to see. In every moment and through every needle on their branches they transmit the memory of eternal truths.

Succulent

The succulents are dedicated to bringing up the Mother's juices and transmitting Her messages of play and relaxation, joy, letting go, and song or dance. They can be found in the regions of Earth connected to the child and they are impassioned in their embrace and healing of inner and outer child nature and consciousness.

DIVISIONS BY GIFTS

Fruit Trees

The fruit-tree families, like the evergreens, are also dedicated to creating and transmitting memories of the eternal, but they are particularly focused on the fulfillment aspect of the Divine Plan. They bring memories and teachings about the Beloved—both the Divine Beloved and the one specific beloved in form created for each of you. They will help you with any and all confusions about love relationships and will bring you to the highest levels of both wisdom and bliss in this regard. They particularly enjoy being tasted and merging with the human form who eats of them. They teach union lessons and their creations, or fruit, are especially focused on taste and scent. This group is particularly joyful in their work. They have a strong connection to the left deep heart, the intensity of love, province of the divine feminine.

Nut Trees

The nut bearers are dedicated to nourishment of the inner child at the deepest levels. One day the connection of nuts to the limbic system, the ancient emotional system in the heart and brain, will be known. The creative force of nut bearers is dedicated to healing the inner child, who feels abandoned by love and lost in darkness, and to freeing the inner spirit child from its casing of fear. They hold transformative forces that work deeply, slowly, and powerfully to bring to the surface the child's joy, security, and divine gifts in love. Nut forces are particularly helpful through the dark nights of the soul and in protecting and sustaining the inner child and helping the child's spiritual power to blossom.

Wood

These trees, which create wood for people to use in architecture, furniture, and crafts, are dedicated to dealing with structure and form. They have a great deal to teach about architecture and geometry, particularly as these relate to sacred geometry, for any who are open to listen. They especially enjoy opening the connection of heart to mind: forming the household structures that hold, surround, and comfort humanity, and making paper products (every page in the books you read is assiduously making links to your heart as you read the ideas written there). These trees could be called the law givers, for they uphold and teach divine law. They are especially connected to the right heart, the divine masculine, as he brings divine law out into the world. It is no accident that these trees are used in the making of books to hold all forms of knowledge. There is a subset of wood-making trees that is concerned with beauty; these offer themselves for the pages of books connected with creative writing, poetry, and song, which are more closely connected to the left heart.

Leaf

These trees are the breathers of the Holy Spirit and are dedicated to the service of the Mother. They transmit Her teachings of harmony, oneness, and the interconnectedness of All. They carry messages about mutual respect, peace, and goodwill among men. They work quite closely with angelic realms and offer very specific transmissions to people based on the requests of people's guardian angels or devic guides. While all trees do this, some are primarily dedicated to this task. Trees whose creative force offers itself to humanity in the form of leaf have healing properties. Some of the healing power is in the etheric or light force, and some is in the physical leaf itself. The venation of leaves will tell you directly what area of the human physical form the tree is dedicated to helping. Ginkgo, for instance, with parallel venation (see glossary), is especially helpful in opening the root chakra and bringing the kundalini/mother creative force into the entire physical system. All leaves with palmate venation (see glossary) are dedicated to opening the flow of love from the heart to action in the outer world, working to heal blocks in the shoulders, arms, and hands especially. Leaves with pinnate venation (see glossary) help to heal the spine and the electrical flow of love coming through it into the deep heart.

Every leaf is dedicated to the human heart and to communicating the abundance of love to all humanity, working primarily through breath.

Bark

In addition to its medicinal qualities, bark has its own way of breathing and transmitting. It is particularly dedicated to healing the masculine aspect of the heart with teachings about making connections from the deep heart to the outer world, holding one's center in turmoil, and staying strongly aligned with the pure axis of love coming into the spine. All these aspects belong to the province of the inner masculine. Most bark varieties have powerful medicinal uses, many of which are unknown to humanity. We would be overjoyed to give these teachings to a person with the purity and patience to listen and transcribe for us. The bark of all trees is closely connected to the medical profession and holds in particular prayerful embrace the medical doctors and nurses of humanity. Bark is also closely connected to the dog family, that is also dedicated to healing the inner masculine, but at the inner child level. The trunks of all trees, in particular the elder trees, hold the stewardship of all plant kingdoms. They await humanity arriving at maturity and taking over this function.

Root

The root forces are quite potent in bringing hidden spiritual depths to the surface. They are in close connection to the etheric light network or grid of light just below the surface all across the Earth. They are also immersed in the watery ethers of the Cosmic Mother as She interpenetrates the seas and juices of Earth's body. They are particularly dedicated to the Great Mother and serve Her in creating powerfully transformative substances that transmit the Mother's laws through water, such as in baths and teas. They are fully focused on the transformation of humanity into the embodiment of these laws, found in the Celtic Vows stated in chapter 1. Roots are the support system for the entire tree and are crucial to the life of everyone. Plants experience physical pain when roots are damaged, which can be moderated by a tree or plant system if it receives prior notice of two hours. The above-ground aspects of trees generally do not feel physical pain. They do have initial emotional pain when damaged or cut, but this is quickly healed by nature. It is most important that people ask permission and work directly with a tree or plant consciousness when harvesting or disturbing its roots. In every sense, the roots are the foundation of all that the tree kingdom offers to humanity and to Earth.

These are the barest details about the wealth of offerings the tree kingdom creates continuously for the healing and comfort of humanity. Because this book is concerned with Druid lore and ascension to wisdom levels, we will say no more. Please know that each tree is fully dedicated to every one of you, and each will be your active friend and teacher should you choose to communicate or develop a relationship with one or more of them. We are honored to serve.

Each person has a very strong affinity with three tree families. Each person's soul once lived within these tree forms and its soul purpose is closely related to theirs. It would help if each and every one of you would go inside and feel which trees are your particular spiritual brothers, for these remember you, watch over you, and are especially dedicated to the mission toward which you are working. They can become pure and caring teachers for everyone in this world who is still so full of pain and mistrust. Every tree, whether in your own family or not, will do its utmost to be your guide and friend. No tree will ever do you harm, for we have only a peaceful embracing love to give to all. May peace and love prevail on Earth. May the holy family be born in you all, as soon as may be, for the establishment, honor, and glory of God's Kingdom on Earth.

YOUR TREE BROTHERS AND SISTERS IN SERVICE TO THE ONE

THE DRUID TREE SYSTEM: THE PATH OF ASCENSION THROUGH SOUL AND SPIRIT REALMS INTO WISDOM

All Druid lore and tradition is dedicated to the ascension of mankind and the establishment of Heaven on Earth to the full realization of the Holy Mother–Father's Kingdom here.

To fully explain the tree path we must digress into the 128 planes of form and the fourteen Logos levels. Each soul and spirit has descended through these in its separation from the One and in building its own separate identity and consciousness, which is the sole purpose of this descent. The Celtic tree path will faithfully lead the seeker up through the planes of soul and spirit in close alignment with the lunar/solar gestational cycle, back to the Great Mother's Womb. The Celts called Her realm the Otherworld, a place where love rules and spirits are joyful and free. The Otherworld will become a reality on Earth as soon as all humanity attains its wisdom status and the veils between worlds disappear. Then all beings in all worlds will become visible to one another again. The Celtic ascension path is divided into three parts. The initial fifteen trees, plus Samhain, take the initiate through the soul planes, facing and transmuting all fears that block the qualities of love and embodying them within the soul. The Ogham symbol from the Druid alphabet is given along with the twenty-four-day moon in which the soul force predominates and the consonant whose sound brings this quality of love into breath. Each of these affect the soul force in all beings.

Please note that the lunar cycle begins at sunset. Samhain and midwinter, while part of the annual calendar, are not numbered because the geometries of the soul forces and templates follow a pattern of fifteen and because they are overlighted by Goddess and God, whose forces affect all aspects of the self, not only the soul.

The next five trees mark the hidden forces that come through the star system Sirius. This is the portal between sensate and soul realms, where all rays from the soul, spirit, and Logos levels enter the physical realms. These five forces are on an annual calendar as well, but the cycle is longer and is marked by the Celtic festival days of Imbolc, Beltane, Lughnasa, and Samhain, for these gateways of growth were clearly felt and known to the Druids. These five forces are those that maintain the time-space fabric of the sensate realms. They are powerful indeed—intense waves of force from all spirit planes and the nine outer Logos levels, which sustain the life force and the spiritual evolution of all beings in the eighteen sensate planes. The geometries are pentagonal. The Ogham symbol of the druid alphabet, the period when each force predominates, and the vowel sound that brings each force into breath are given for each tree.

After this come the five Logos forces associated with the mystical path, the inner five Logos planes that draw the initiate into a co-creative partnership with God/Goddess. These forces affect the innermost spirit of each being and draw each back into a loving union and ongoing partnership with the Beloved and Creator levels of the Logos. This partnership never ends—that is, one cannot ascend beyond the Creator levels of the Logos—for it sets up a close and cyclical partnership of growth and love with higher and higher levels of love expressed from the Logos through each person. It is a true love partnership, and such partnerships are the most powerful forces in the universe. Their geometries are based on the number five, but in a star form, indicating the outer expression of the pentagon.

Of the trees that guide us, the King and Queen trees are those that reach to the center point of the Logos and carry energies down from that level. The Pillar trees reach to the five inmost Logos planes, and the Noble trees reach to the nine outermost Logos planes and spirit levels. Whether a specific tree family is Pillar or Noble is indicated in the list of the twenty-five tree guides to Celtic ascension below. Each plane is affiliated with one tree family, but we will be discussing only the twenty-five of the Druid system, plus Samhain and midwinter. All trees have central etheric channels reaching to the plane from which they were created and with which they are associated. Each embodies the specific geometries and teachings of this level, or plane, and breathe these, through bark and leaf, into the air. Trees are the keepers of the Holy Spirit on Earth and bring highly refined energies onto the planet. The current destruction of certain species, such as the ancient conifers, is distorting both the Holy Spirit here and the consciousness of Her on Earth.

THE TWENTY-FIVE TREE GUIDES TO CELTIC ASCENSION INTO THE MOTHER-FATHER'S KINGDOM

1. Birch, **December 22–January 15, the letter *B* or Beth, Pillar Tree.** Please note that the twenty-four-day lunar cycle begins at sunset. The birch is the tree of new beginnings. It creates from sunlight and water—as do all trees—a very pure clear ray, which infuses the human friend with hope and new possibilities. It holds the memory of love once experienced by the spirit at the very highest levels of eternal realms, the memory of Christ/Magdalene as the Beloved. The birch family breathes onto Earth a sweet breath of God, as all trees do. Its sap contains a concentrated form of the same essence, as does smoke from a birch-log fire. The essence, when taken in by a new initiate on the path, will open the heart's deep longing to return to love, the pure love of God as the Beloved. It floods the pilgrim with the hope of becoming purified and returning Home. It is most active in the twenty-four days following the midwinter solstice, when the light seeds of the next lunar/solar cycle of growth have been implanted in the womb of each initiate. The birch family wishes to thank humanity for cherishing birch in all its forms, and to state its great joy in this service to Mother Earth and humankind. The birch streams from the Homestar plane.

2. Rowan or Mountain Ash, January 16–February 8, the letter *L* or Luis, Pillar Tree. Rowan is the tree of the Father. It creates breath, sap, wood, and berries containing the greatheartedness and protectiveness of the Father, as well as His guiding hand. Less well known is His matchmaking tendency, which is most evident in the berries. The breath and essence of this tree create a protective cloud that does indeed keep evil forces barred. It holds the memory of the True Father, the Lion Heart, King of Heaven, with His great love for all His many children. This tree is a particular comfort to any who have been harmed by a father or father figure and is a great healer of such wounds. Its effect is most pronounced in the twenty-four–day lunar cycle of late January and early February. It holds the sprouts of growth, newly birthed at Imbolc, in its protective love and is especially joyful in this service to humanity.

3. Ash, February 9–March 4, the letter *N* or Nion, Pillar Tree. The ash is the great world tree. Its light channel reaches to the highest realms of Heaven and it breathes out the memory of the fairy realms, the joyful memory of the child spirit as it romped among the gardens, flowers, and cherubs, and created as it willed. This tree essence in sap, leaf, wood, and breath is the freedom of the child to create beauty and love in the security of a world of nothing but love, where harm never gains a toehold. It is closely connected to the blue-sky realms and will open any ailments of breath and lungs. It is active in late February and early March when the child's excitement grows for the development of the year to come. The ash family is so happy to hold this sweet tenderness for the child within.

4. Alder, March 5–March 28, the letter *F* or Fearn. The alder family is most connected to the minnow or to fish in general. It is the little boy's wriggly energy, which is added to his dreams for growth that have gestated within him and is ready to move into form or action in the outer world as spring approaches. This energy brings the pure energy of the male sperm to the mixture of creativity, giving the initiate the force needed to put the year's goals into form. Alder is a watery essence drawn directly from the inner belly of the Earth Mother, the raw potentiality She holds there. It makes the inner sap of a person run and will help to heal any blocks to action that you may face within yourself. Alder foundations do indeed carry great spurts of energy to the structures built above them. They are very closely connected to the Mother and the cosmic ethers, the fish families, and the salty seas.

5. Black Willow, March 29–April 21, the letter *S* or Saille, Pillar Tree. These river willows bring the pure flow of love that is found in fresh water streaming from the Great Mother. Their channels reach to the Logos and carry down the silver stream, which regulates the flow of pure love from the Great Queen of Heaven. Her sap in particular will heal all heartache and all disorders of the watery bodily systems. She will bring comfort and relief from pain, the Mother's great concern for all Her children. This black willow is the Earth Mother tree. Her juices will help to heal wounds to the inner mother, especially the depletion and servitude the human mother bears so strongly. She welcomes all who wish to sit beneath her comforting, accepting presence. It is no accident that Easter most often falls within her province. This tree is especially connected to the black mother, who has opened her heart to children of all colors in acceptance of all.

6. White Hawthorne, April 22–May 15, the letter *H* or Huath. This is the tree of cleansing and is closely connected with lightning storms, which clear areas that are in severe imbalance with the inner child. The creations of this tree will do the same, usually through a disruption or disturbance in the initiate's life that signals he or she is approaching a state dangerous to the child spirit. Hawthornes make shadow reflections quite active and the necessity for responsibility becomes very clear. Hawthorne is closely connected to the thymus and the immune system and creates, along with the qualities of fierce protectiveness, deep longing for purity at any cost and the essential holiness of all things. It prepares the vessel for the return of the Beloved. The members of the Hawthorne family have been much misunderstood as bearers of evil and doers of harm, and they wish to state clearly that they are the sacred protectors of deep holiness and their efforts have maintained such hidden holiness for ages. They hope this purity of purpose will now be understood. Their wish is only to bless, for clearing work brings in the great rewards of love and abundance.

7. Oak, May 16–June 8, the letter *D* or Duir, the Great King Tree. The oak brings the memory and essence of the Beloved, the Christ stream. It floods the land with the memory of the eternal, where each being was pure Christ essence; each was paired with his or her one true beloved and each served his or her partner as priest or priestess of God, as the Beloved of All. The oak is the Arthurian tree. He comes as world server to unify and embrace all in his great heart of love and only love. His breath, sap, and wood are particularly healing to the masculine and carry the imprint of the Celtic code as stated in chapter 1. He is the overseer of the forest kingdom, and brings his intimate and tender love to all creatures great and small. His light channel reaches to the very center point of the celestial and carries the highest vibration from those realms. All who have lost hope of a partnership in love: See the oak. He will remind you of the truth. His power knows *no bounds*.

8. Holly, June 9–July 2, the letter *T* or Tinne, Noble Tree. The holly is the tree of fierce protectiveness of those who are weak and laden with heavy loads. This tree creates breath and leaf that carry the quality of balance in battle along with a willingness to give one's life to preserve the safety and good laws of the Kingdom. These are the great gifts of the masculine. The holly and its cousins, the fierce spruces, will shore up any who are in danger of collapse in the face of evil or great fear. They will teach you to hold your balance and your power of personal choice in the face of great pain. This is the tree of the spiritual warrior and all are proud to strengthen those who are floundering in their battles against evil.

9. Hazel, July 3–July 26, the letter *C* or Coll, Noble Tree. The hazel brings the flowering of prophecy and intuition, in particular, the great gifts of the feminine. It brings the flow of the feminine as she begins turning toward the inward spiral of the year. The gifts of the hazel are those of the priestess, one who can see and hear clearly those of the spirit realm and follow their directions for bringing forth the Father's Kingdom on Earth. Her heart is closely aligned with the Father's and with His wish for all beloveds to find one another and know the bliss of love forever true. She has a sweet nature and a tenderness for those forlorn of true love and will gently direct these people in their lessons of opening to partnership in love on their return Home. She can bring great clarity of inner vision and hearing and open connection to the spirit realms, for she is most able to walk in both worlds—the sensate and soul/spirit realms—at once. Her quality is kindness to all, no matter how low or lofty each may be.

10. Apple, July 27–August 19, the letter Q or Quert, the Great Queen Tree. Apple is the Great Queen of Heaven, bride of the oak and beloved of Christ. Her essence carries the full memory of the feminine receiving her Christ within at all levels, the union of the highest order, the Magdalene stream. She is pure in her adoration of the masculine beloved, untiring in her service to His cause on Earth, and full of the rich maturity and beauty of womanhood. Her fruit, in particular, will bring the memory of union with the Christ Beloved before the descent, the most intimate of loves, and will spark a deep and intense longing for the experience of this union. Her energies want union at every level—spirit, soul, and sense—and in all fields— mental, emotional, and physical. She will settle for nothing less. She is the great lover on Earth, sensuous, seductive, elegant, and holy, consort of Christ. It is Her influence that anchors the dreams and actions from the first half of the year to full manifestation in the harvest.

11. Vine, August 20–September 12, the letter *M* or Muin, Noble Tree. Tree of the grape, vine bears the sweet intoxication of love fulfilled. It imprints the full memory of satiation, the ecstasy of love's embrace, and the celestial kingdom where beloveds live in complete union. Its fruit can be a dangerous thing, for its seduction can cause a person to forget all else in his or her longing for such love. It is best used sparingly, with reverence and the cooperation of the sacred. This is the time of harvest, when the fruits of earlier months' labor begin to be felt and enjoyed in the physical world. The vine family would like to request that humanity be more careful, asking permission before using its fruit and considering a less grasping approach. They ask this politely and with concern for the internal damage some of you sustain in misusing its fruit, for this effect severely saddens them.

12. Ivy, September 13–October 6, the letter *G* or Gort. The ivy family brings the quality of tenacity in the face of great suffering, the patient endurance of the feminine in birthing her Divine Child, and the invincible refusal to give up in the face of extreme hardship or harm. This is the great gift of the feminine in form, and usually involves some sacrifice, particularly the female sacrifice of years of life devoted to others in selfless service to the All. Ivy is also deeply connected to the black race and the feminine in all, who, no matter how many times she is knocked down or destroyed, will forever rise in her tender unshakable spiral of life. The ivy family can teach invincibility in great hardship and great pain, the long suffering endurance of the descended feminine. Her beauty is truly divine.

13. Reed or Cattail, October 7–October 30, the letter *Ng* or Ngetal, Noble Tree. The reed family represents a global community or family, a return to the Mother, where all operate under and in service to the laws of love. Fear is unknown; there is celebration of a job well done and its fruits are enjoyed by all together, of one heart and mind and at one table. This family transmits the peace of Heaven attained, the joining together of all beings into one great family of loving support in unified praise to the Mother and Father of All. This tree is ever closely connected to the watery flow of the Mother's love and can bring a gentle, sustained inner and outer peace.

14. Blackthorn, October 31–November 23, the letter *Z* or *St* or Straif, Noble Tree. Blackthorn is the tree of transformation. It can take you from one plane to another, from one form to another. It will lead you directly into the darkness of the unrevealed to bring through your deepest desire. This is the midnight tree, the one to which you can give your most secret longing. It can take your request into the depths of the Mother's Womb and bring forth Her thickest and most powerful creative force to make your wish become reality. Its time is the time to make your Christmas wishes known, for the spirit world will rally to provide your most intimate desires. The coalescing of energies for the year to come begins at this time, as does the tying off of all loose ends for the creations of the year before in preparation for the rest and comfort of winter's time of holding within the Mother's Womb. The Blackthorn family wishes to state that they, too, have been much maligned as bringers of evil, when in actuality their truth is to be the magic wand for humankind. They are joyful in their deep and ancient wisdom in the ways of magic in service to love and wish it to be known that they particularly enjoy manifesting beloveds into form. They also wish to state that any and all requests of them are taken with utmost respect and seriousness in sacred service.

• **Five intercessory days, November 24–November 28.** This is the time of recycling. The old forms for the passing year are rapidly broken down and returned to pure potentiality for the creations of the new cycle. This phase is connected with the moon and does not have a tree representative. The tree kingdom surrenders to The One Great Mother of All during these days. Her power is in full force and the veil between worlds is indeed very thin.

15. Elder, November 29–December 20, the letter *R* or Ruis, Noble Tree. The wisdom lessons gained from the past year's experience are deeply anchored into the physical, emotional, and mental systems at all levels during this phase. These gifts are eternal and enter the wisdom structure of the feminine. They will stay with that evolving form for all eternity and will determine the final level the spirit returns to upon departing from Earth at death. These great lessons of love can only be anchored into the structure of the mind, emotions, and senses through the experience of living and are the true and most highly treasured gifts of The Great Mother. It is Her gift to all who develop a separate identity, and Her greatest wish is that these wisdom lessons be embodied in all who walk the path, the labyrinth of experience and life in this world. The Elder family will help anchor any such lessons learned in your deepest levels and will help resolve any confusion into its highest resolution in wisdom. They are grateful for the opportunity to serve and full of a sweet compassion for all who suffer to achieve their wisdom status and full independence as separate creators in love. Like the vine, they ask that their wine be used in moderation and with a view toward the sanctity of these embodiments.

• **Midwinter solstice.** Midwinter marks the beginning of the new annual cycle, when the pure seeds of light come, with the rising sun, into all forms from highest Heaven and anchor deeply into the womb of the feminine within to repeat once again the gestation cycle of experiential manifestation.

Five Hidden Cyclic Forces, Vowels, Pillar Trees All

The following are the trees of the hidden wheel. These are the forces that keep the spiral of time and the cycles of growth turning, the ray forces that hold open the portal from spirit realms and create the vast spatial bowl for the time-space fabric. It is their cyclic pushing or torsion that brings through the onward flow of love within space and time and it is through this portal that all light, all creator power, all love streams into the physical realm. These are the hidden streams connected to the five basic phases of transformation, the lunar side of the lunar/solar year.

There are ten divisions within each of these five cyclic forces, together comprising the fifty rowers of the Sirian star system. This portal to spirit realms goes directly through the Sirian system, and upon it all life, all time, and all space depend. It is the central axis or stream coming from the center point of the Logos into all physical worlds. This cosmic bowl is the One Goddess, Magdalene, Mother of All.

Long *A* predominates from midwinter to Imbolc, February 5, and takes a pilgrim through the gateway of birth. Long *O* carries the impulse from Imbolc to Beltane, May 5, which is the gateway where male and female come together into full action. Long *U* moves from Beltane to Lughnasa, August 5, the gateway where the joining of forces in the active phase begins to give way. Long *E* predominates from Luhgnasa through the sweet days of harvest and the breaking down of the current year's partnership to the gateway of Samhain, November 24. Double *I,* or *II,* moves through this five-day breakdown transit to the new cycle, and *I* or *Y* pushes to the gateway of the midwinter solstice or implantation. The year is a sweet dance of love in all its many aspects. Each of these phases reaches its crescendo at the appropriate equinox or solstice, for all are on the slow ocean wave of the Mother's flow. She is so happy to bring your dreams and desires into birth, with and for each of you.

16. Elm, new year impulse, the letter *A* or Ailm. The elm family stands tall and graceful. It holds the grace of the feminine in her full sovereignty, her regal form in full possession of her powers of intuition, self-choice, and grace. The disease that has ravaged the elm is a clear message from nature to humanity of the state of the sovereign feminine in your time. But she will rise again. Her symbol is a golden crown, a simple circlet of the eternal love of the stately feminine in her prime.

17. Gorse, vernal equinox impulse, the letter *O* or Onn. The gorse family represents the struggle and the sweetness of growth. It knows how to deal with obstacles, it knows the toughness of pushing forward in adversity and harvesting the sweet perfume of spirit grown into a new beauty and strength. The essence of the gorse is strength and sweetness combined, and it is very closely linked to the Earth, for this bittersweet quality marks all streams of Earth so far. Gorse will grow under the harshest of conditions and do the hard work of growth, flowering in conscious beauty. The Gorse family wishes to state that its spines are not meant to harm you and would like to correct this misperception. These spines hold an essence that can bring great strength in standing up to foes or forces that would block one's inner gifts and are a gift in pure service to mankind.

18. Heather, the summer solstice impulse, the letter *U* or Ur. The heather is a lowly plant that grows along glens and heights. It is found in places of wildness and freedom and brings the breath of the rose light of love. This plant represents the wildness and heights of love expressed, the far-reaching expanse that can be transformed by the gifts of love given freely. It brings forth the wild freedom of love: wild joy, wild passion, the wonderful depth that love can bring to bear, a most magical plant.

19. Aspen, the autumnal equinox impulse, the letter *E* or Edad. The aspen family brings the grace of love in its fulfillment, the victory won, the soft whispering of love that has satisfied itself in accomplishing its goals of expression through the year's active phase. It has a quietness of sharing, an overflow of love that spills into the family and community and calls for gratitude, praise, and celebration. It is the tree of harvest after a job well done. The aspen will help you to keep yourselves steady and focused until the goal is achieved and the struggle gives way to pleasure. It is a tree of pleasure and clarity of purpose. Purposefulness and victory are its essence. The aspen family wishes to state that the general belief in it as the tree of overcoming implies far too much struggle and hardship than is actually experienced, and would like you to receive the softness and joy that it brings as well. It is a tree particularly happy in its work.

20. Yew, the birth pushing impulse, the letter *Y* or *I* or Idad.
Yew is the tree of rebirth—specifically the English yew, for the other cultivars hold variations that have mingled with other streams. The English Yew holds the ancient truths that each spirit was born in pure holiness and to pure holiness it will always return. Its roots draw from the Womb of the Mother, deep in the Earth, and bring Her creative forces into play. These are powerful transforming juices that break down the old, the no longer useful, and open the way to new adventures of love awaiting the initiate in the cycle of the year to come. The yew is the pregnant Womb of the Mother, ever in service to co-create into physical reality and emotional experience the desires of all Her children with great love and untiring eternal effort. It is deeply secure in its powers to gestate into form and is the tree of manifestation of desires at the deepest level, into the purest and holiest of forms. Its overall goal is to rebirth the Christ in all, so truth and joy will reign forever and seal the door where evil dwells, now and forevermore. Its stream is the most ancient of the feminine, and holding your deepest desires in love and pregnant power is its own deepest joy and expression of love. The yew dearly loves you all, each and every one.

• **Mistletoe, midwinter solstice impulse, the letter *J*.** The Mistletoe plant represents the seeds of the divine implanted into the womb of the feminine Earth on midwinter sunrise and into the inner feminine of all beings. It is not included among the tree forms in the Celtic system because it streams directly from the Father. Mistletoe brings the tiniest symbols of light, the DNA of what will be created in the year to come, sent from the Father's Heart straight to each of you. These are His most cherished wishes and gifts for each of you, blessings of the highest order inseminated into the Mother's great, loving Womb. Mistletoe is revered above all plants, for its fruit holds the Holiest of Holies, the seeds of transformation of the Earth into Her true Heavenly form, restoration of the Father's Kingdom in union with the wisdom gained through the Mother's life of experience. It brings the true experience of creativity and divinity, the most intimate union of divine male and female. Midwinter is the most sacred day of the druid year and is held in the highest reverence, for intimate union of male and female at all levels of spirit, form, and sense is the highest experience of the bliss of love revealed. We of the Druid order wish this exquisite fulfillment, union of spirit and sense, the true meaning of hue-man, or light and body, for all beings now journeying toward that happy end. May you all live happily ever after and know the fairy tale of love come true, each and every one of you, as speedily as may be. So be it and hurrah.

Trees of the Five Inmost Logos Planes, the Mystical Path

And, finally, come the five hidden streams of the inner five Logos planes, Noble trees all.

21. Grove, midwinter to vernal equinox, the letter *K* or Koad. Koad brings the force of a group whose spirits, souls, and hearts are working in unity. It is the symbol of the spirit family and the power of such a force remains untapped on Earth. This is the power of the clan or tribe. As communities of spirit families begin to form in the near future here, this force will begin to rise and be felt. There are tree forces linked to each of the great Celtic clans, as in the Douglas fir or the Fraser fir. These groves wait to unite and transfer their great powers to these future families and communities.

22. Spindle, vernal equinox to summer solstice, the letter *Oi* or Oir. The spindle tree is the tree of cycles, the long cycles set into place by the Great Mother of All in Her tapestry of life. These cycles will take each spirit out of the realms of light into the wild adventure of physical life through the creation of a separate identity, then up the steep travail of the wisdom teachings, and into full separate creator-hood. It is a glorious dance and it is the Mother Herself who weaves the turns and twists of physical reality and of life, who leads each on their way. It is She, the Great Womb of life, who gives this gift of physical manifestation to all who obtain purity of heart, mind, and body. To Her be the glory of it. Hurrah!

23. Honeysuckle, summer solstice to fall equinox, the letter *Ui* or Uilleand. The honeysuckle is the tree of the Divine Child suckling from the breast of the Great Mother of All. For it is She who births all life in form and She who is the container for all physical worlds. It is the milk of Her love that flows from the Godhead and into every heart in all forms. She is the source of love itself: love of life, love of form, love of beauty, love of expression, love of body. Honeysuckle is the embodiment of these loves to which it gives expression, all the variety of loves that can be felt only in the physical and are entirely unknown in spirit worlds. Its gifts are richly diverse and overflowing with joy and abundance for everyone.

24. Beech, fall equinox to Samhain, the letter *Ph* or Phagos. The beech is the seat of the most ancient wisdom. This tree holds the memory of paradise, but, more than that, it keeps selected memories of union, the exquisite union of male and female that was known and anchored deeply within each heart to keep the longing and certainty of love that would bring each one Home at last. The time for opening these sweetest of memories is here. Rejoice and drink in the sweet fulfillment. This tree holds the Goddess's finest gift to each of you, the experience of union with God/Goddess in the physical, the Arthurian fulfillment.

25. The Sea or Mor, Samhain to midwinter. The sound is the endless ebb and flow of the cosmic sea, the sound of the tides, the sound that can be heard by holding a shell to your ear. The sea is the Great Cosmic Mother Herself, the Magdalene, Bride of Christ. It is She who spreads Herself into the cosmos and She who holds the space, accepting all suffering and all pain and recycling each form into pure pregnant possibility for future creations in love. It is She who works in partnership with the Cosmic Christ to take in His seed and move the cosmic tides forward to the rebirth of all in His Image. She has given and given and given and Her love and strength are *infinite*.

We would simply like to add that Her depletion and fatigue are great and humanity would do well to honor and serve the One who gives them life. Her powers, Her love, Her beauty are unsurpassable. To Her be the Kingdom and the glory as soon as may be.

The tree kingdom stands together, all the families that, in their varied gifts to all humankind, serve the Mother in Her land of experience here. We wish you to understand and to receive our great love for you, each and every one. We honor you for your suffering, as you take on the shroud of pain to birth yourselves into a full experience of divinity. We see the rapid approach of the dawn of light across this beloved planet Earth and we rejoice with you in the coming end of your travail. We are willing to work doubly, even triply hard, in easing the remaining time of transition and turmoil. We seek any who wish to approach us, who are willing to listen and co-create with us, whether in blends of essences or medicines or specific breathing release work. We look forward with a deep and eager anticipation to the renewal of brotherhood with all humankind. We cheer the arrival of love purified after wisdom lessons are embodied by all and look forward with particular joy to the co-creation of works in pure love.

One suggestion is being made now that could become a reality in a very short time and would do much to heal the inner child. We would be willing to have varieties of our families planted in a tree park, so to speak, a tree playground. It would be possible for the spirit tree forms to reveal themselves and hold the child in a physical way, as we did so long ago in celestial realms, if this request is made and the energies are held in love and the work is accomplished by one or two individuals who feel so inclined. This would go a long way toward healing the deep grief of the inner child, who feels this separation so intensely.

Be blessed, all humankind. Know that we serve our Divine Mother and Father and you. We have only love to give you from our deepest hearts. Let us join hands in loving partnership once again. A rousing cheer for love in all its forms! Hurrah!

❧ 4 ❧
The Stone People:
Astrologers

We are the true representatives of all star systems on your Earth. We contain the physical structures and the capacity to transmit, magnify, and connect you to all star systems and the Logos in this universe and beyond. Humanity considers Earth to be a separate entity unto itself, but this is not so, for the bones or bedrock of Earth and Her molten inner crystalline structures are closely linked to multiple star systems. Your planet is a composite of stardust, star crystal grains from the far reaches of this universe. There are a select few minerals that even reach to the other six parallel evolving universes and to the central organizing Paradisiacal universe. These will be explained.

We, the stone creations, are the true elders of your planet, for we hold the memories of your descent, all the way to the beginning, and can transmit thought and emotion from those star systems and from your original family members with ease and with great joy. It is our privilege to transmit these joyful memories. As the trees work primarily through breath and the watery systems of the physical body, we work primarily through light, capturing and focalizing the rising and waning astrological rays coming into play to move forward the rush of love as it cycles from form to form. You could think of each of us as a magnifying glass, each type with a different structural grid and ray color that attune it and make it a natural focalizer for specific rays of love. There are 140 separate rays, each with its own quality of love. The permutations and blends are innumerable. The deepest joy of the stone kingdom is to remind you of your star essence, that you are all star children of the One, and as full of dignity, light, and potential as any great star in the night sky. Indeed, you will each attain your stardom before you depart the Earth plane, and we are your spotlights, your footlights, and your cheering section on that leg of your journey. We are much more closely connected with you than nearly all of you know.

Our radiations of the various lights of love are sent into the carbon and silicate crystals of your bones, which are crystalline in nature. Your bones are exact replicas of the star systems in this universe and each has definite affinities for various parts of the cosmic sky. You are a star child, a composite of carbon and silicate crystals, and you can consciously capture and co-create very powerfully with these rays of light. Our scribe and author has requested to bring through this science and her request will be honored, and is, in fact, one of the seeds implanted for her in this and the next solar cycles. We welcome all who wish to work with her or wish to approach us independently, so that we can blend our desires for the creation of higher gifts and expressions of love. We will eagerly co-create with all who come to us in purity and respect and who will actively work to bring through such creations. The rays of light are of the Father's Kingdom, as the tree creations are the breath and the watery systems of the Mother. Stone is very closely connected to bone, to the sacred geometry of the building of form, and the transformations that can be achieved through combinations of such structural forms and light rays. It is a powerful science, more powerful than humanity is now aware. You have just barely begun to tap into this power in the infancy of your computer technology. Again, we are most joyful to work with any seeker in co-creating new and astronomically more powerful computer chips, for all those whose desires are truly based in love. We will not serve the pursuit of individual power or money in any form or to the slightest degree, however.

There are twelve basic families of stone or crystal, and these divisions are all based on their internal geometry or structure. These families bring rays from the twelve Logos planes into all lower worlds. It is this structure that is the most important in determining the task of each stone family, for it is this structure through which a stone or crystal has chosen to serve one of the lords of the rays. We serve simply by aiming the unseen forces or light streams through our tiny geometrical structures into each world. We can draw rays into ourselves, focus and aim these rays through our geometrical lenses, and increase or decrease the speed of the photons streaming through our inner lensworks. The rays or forces of love, as they spread through all worlds, create the blends of emotion in the ethers surrounding everyone and powerfully activate emotions within. These influences can be planetary, individual, or anything in between. It is impossible not to feel or be emotionally moved by our radiations, and it is these unseen forces, for light and love are primarily a force with both intent and purpose, that create and move forward the dramas and personal unfoldment of all worlds. These unseen influences are the God/Goddess force of love revealed to you here and are the most powerful influences in the universe. They do not fail to have their effect.

All star systems step down the radiation from the Logos for use in the lower worlds. Pure radiation would evaporate many life forms and is forbidden. We are the crystalline grids that focalize these rays, then transduce, and aim them in the appropriate direction. There are vast unseen networks of structure through that the various worlds are held. It is these invisible geometric grids which hold the space between the many planes of form. These are the simplest understandings, but there are other nettings of geometry that serve the great mystery but they are beyond the scope of this short work. This information relating to the unrevealed, dark matter of the universe will be given to one who is of a particularly peaceful and spiritual inner nature, if there is one who is so inclined.

There are seven lords of rays within the Great Creator Logos; the basic trinity of Mother, Father, and Child rays; and the Christ ray and the One Beloved at the inmost levels—twelve in all. We will briefly describe these twelve families of stone and their uses, their connections to the sacred planets, and their home star systems.

Here is how the Logos rays unfold each individual: The beam of the gold ray creates the two aspects of male and female within. All individuals have both aspects, which do not fully separate and are not considered separate individuals. Then the inner lights of mind, heart, and body form under the beams of the three-in-One. The three great rays of aspect then form the inner structures of mother, father, and child. Following this, the seven lesser rays of aspect form the light body of each individual, which looks precisely like a rainbow. Each of the twelve rays has precise powers to open and unfold each of the twelve chakras of each person, and the ray lords are the guardians of the development or unfoldment of these various aspects of every person. Without these light geometries beamed into all worlds through the mineral kingdom, all structure of the universe and each individual would collapse. In the descriptions below, the love quality, Logos plane, ray color, and geometric shape for each stone and crystal family is noted.

TWELVE LOGOS PLANES: FAMILIES OF STONE AND CRYSTAL, RAY COLOR, AND LIGHT STRUCTURE

1. The One Beloved, thirteenth Logos plane; ray color is gold; structure is a point. This is the Father's Kingdom, where all forms live in intimate loving partnership with their beloved and recognize themselves as temples and servers to their partner in bringing through this highest form of love and intimacy from the Heart of Hearts. The Mother rules here in equal power, but because of Her descent with the child and Her active presence in lower worlds, Her energies are not currently as pronounced as those of the Father. Here there is union of the great Mother-Father's consciousness with all beings at all levels, and this deep union of the consciousness of spirit, soul, and sense is felt between all partners. This is the plane of sweet communion. Mother and Father are known as Isis and Osiris or Christ and Magdalene. The gold ray brings through these rays and remembrances of love once experienced by every individual at that level, and is of particular assistance in all struggles with the beloved. This ray is filtered through the Orion Nebula, birthplace of true love for each and every one of you. We wish you rich pleasure on this journey to your beloved. The gold ray is focalized into your solar system through the sun. It is from the union impulse of the beloved, streaming out into all worlds, that all things are created in pure, passionate, and intimate love of All that is.

2. Three-in-One, ninth Logos plane; ray colors are red, blue, and yellow blended into white; structure is a circle. The second family of structure serves the One or the Three-in-One, for it has a tripartite nature, though the three are carefully blended into a single unit. Ray colors are yellow, blue and red—Father, Mother and Child, respectively. These blend into white and are beamed to Earth through the corona of the Sun. Quartz crystal and other six-sided minerals serve this lord. This force of love is of the softest and gentlest nature, for its essence is to hold All within the One and to radiate pure love to all. It feels like the gentle child heart of your world, where the forces are blended and soft. But, in actuality, it is a perfect blend of the three basic natures, mother, father, and child. It is this ray you invoke when you call forth the Christ into your worship and His/Her presence will feel like a gentle embracing power. Jesus Christ was the highest teacher from this level.

This class of rock will help to heal all of the deepest wounds to the child heart, which is in truth a blend of the three natures as well. These wounds are very severe, and this diffuse ray of love and healing power is most gentle and soft to heal such wounds within the highest perfection of love. The quartz kingdom is so joyous in service to the inner child spirit of humanity and to the child spirit in all realms. We, too, ask for an interested seeker who wishes to work with us, for there is great healing power in pure quartz that has not been discovered, and we are eager to be in greater service to all children suffering in fear. Our ray quality could best be described as tenderness. It streams through the star system Sirius. We love you so.

The Three Great Rays of Aspect

3. The Father, eighth Logos plane; ray color is yellow; structure is a line. Within the heart of the One are the three rays of aspect. First is the Father, with a line structure. This yellow ray brings in the organizing seeds of growth, tiny light symbols or vortexes that have encoded within them the future unfoldment of growth for that form, on both the inner and outer aspects. These tiny vortexes or templates are found in the DNA of all nuclei and are carried along light networks radiated from world to world by this particular family. The ray color is bright yellow and the stone is sulfur crystals. These rays are brought through the Eagle Nebula in the Orion star system and the planet Jupiter. To anyone who is blocked from achieving their highest purpose, this ray can be of great assistance in locating and penetrating those blocks. The rays of this plane are quite focused, and single-pointed penetration through barriers is its specialty. These forces are the trailblazers of the stone kingdom. How much we enjoy our work in helping all see a ray of light through the darkness of despair! We are the keepers and guides through the dark night of the soul and are fully at your service. The greatest teacher from this level was Abraham.

4. The Mother, seventh Logos plane; ray color is blue; structure is a wave. Blue, associated with the Mother, is the second great ray of aspect. It comes through fluorite crystals and basalt, particularly the purer aqua basalt found beneath the black form with which you are most familiar. The structure is a wave. The greatest teacher from this level was Mary, mother of Jesus. This ray is connected to the cosmic ethers, to emotion and oceans. Its influence is gentle and rhythmic and operates within a lunar cyclic motion, which is slow, steady, and fruitful. The qualities of love are patience and diligence, which bear the fruit of the eternal. This ray or force of love is present in all watery forms and in many quasi-crystals of a watery consistency, particularly blood. This ray's nature is particularly kind and fun-loving and is intimate to the mother-child connection, the Mother Mary essence. Its radiation streams through the Great Bear star system, Ursa Major, and the planet Saturn. It is happy to help you in your trials that necessitate the patient endurance needed for full rebirth and to hold all in the gentle cleansing ebb and flow of love. It promotes harmony and a gentle onward movement in the blossoming of love.

5. The Child, sixth Logos plane; ray color is red; structure is a triangle. The third of the great rays of aspect is red, with the structure of a triangle. It is associated with the child and its qualities of love are personal power and drive or force. The greatest teacher at this level was Mohammed. The love force of this plane has a three-sided ray form and moves directly forward. This ray form is present in the granite family and the crystals of smoky quartz and will help any and all whose confidence in their own personal power has been weakened or lost. This ray is responsible for the masculine phallic force and the pure pleasure of being oneself. It is the great confidence booster of the mineral kingdom and streams through the star system Orion and the planet Uranus. It is also the pusher and mover that brings the unrevealed into form and thus moves forward the cosmic force of growth in love. Its grids are the most powerful and the least visible throughout the cosmos and are closely connected to dark matter.

The Seven Lesser Rays of Aspect

The seven rays of aspect are split into: four top rays, one separator ray, and two lower rays as seen in the seven-fold chakra system of the human body and in the seven parallel universes. All planes above these are within the Paradisiacal universe and the Logos.

6. Personal power, sixth Logos plane; ray color is red; structure is a square. The first of the seven rays is bright red. It is closely connected with the personal power of each individual, but blends this with the quality of being physical. It is active in the sensate sheaths and the physical realm. Its quality of love is energy or direct movement toward a goal. This ray, which comes through rubies and the rocks of sandstone, serves in holding together the many within a larger form, such as a community, and will help a group come together into consensus based on the purely personal wills of all involved. It is a good form for resolving group issues. Its structure is a square and it streams through the star system Polaris and the planet Mars. It carries a strong pleasure of being in the physical and can help all who are not loving toward their physical bodies, movement, or physical sensations of any kind. It is also a transducer of the phallic force or the masculine principle. It is the personal will and it will bring all into connection with the personal desires they wish to manifest into physical reality and experience in a physical way. This is the ray of the physical experience of being.

7. Intimacy or creativity, fifth Logos plane; ray color is orange; structure is a crescent. Second of the seven rays of aspect is orange or peach. It signifies the realm of the inner essence or the inner self-creating into the physical. Its structure is a crescent. It is the ray of intimacy, or physical union of the two into one. Its quality of love is intimacy and it is radiated through the moonstone family and through red sandstone. These stones will help transform any and all fears about physical closeness and will heal many sexual distortions. This ray will move each person into an understanding of the great sanctity of this physical act, union of the sacred masculine and feminine within the physical dimension, which is not available to those in spirit form. It is this level, whose power is primarily feminine, that takes the elementals and creates the physical vessel for each individual incarnation of spirit into Earth. Its quality is holding in love and creating in love, associated with the feminine principle and water. It streams through the Pleiades and the planet Venus. The greatest teacher at this level was Teresa of Avila.

8. Consciousness, second Logos plane; ray color is yellow; structure is a four-sided diamond. The third of the seven rays of aspect is bright yellow, the separator ray across the diaphragm. It is the ray of consciousness or thought and is brought through by the constellation Leo and the planet Mercury. Its quality is one of alertness or attention and, combined with focus, it can move mountains. This ray is brought through to Earth by the silica family in mica and chrysolite crystals. These will help in gaining clarity and bringing the preconscious through the barrier of the unconscious into full consciousness. This ray is associated with the various streams of thought of mankind and the various languages. It promotes diversity and full development of the individual self or identity and is a necessary component in growth of all kinds. It serves humanity in her onward march toward gaining knowledge and furthering the potential and the evolution of humankind as a whole in its own direction, separate from all other kingdoms. All silica families beam directly from the Paradisiacal system within the river of the Milky Way or the flow of love from the Great Mother and are particularly nourishing to the inner child and the individual personality. All beaches and all glass windows—all glass of any kind, even bits of rubble that go unnoticed—are actively involved in the freedom of the person and Divine Child process and radiate in every moment. The greatest teacher at this level was Moses.

9. Emotion, fourth Logos plane; ray color is green; structure is a pentagon. The forth of the rays of aspect is green, the great heart ray, which is the ray of the interconnectedness of inner and outer worlds. This ray will teach you that there is not other; you must love others as you love yourself and experience all others as you experience yourself. This ray is brought through the schist granites, marble, and emerald families, the Big Dipper star system, and the planet Earth. These rocks or rays will help you with any and all issues pertaining to matters of the heart and the dilemmas of giving and receiving love at an emotional level. Their service toward the emotional fulfillment of all humankind into the greatest experience of emotional love is their devotion to the All, and they delight in this work. Their grids are quite tricky and changeable, and you must use discernment in making your way through them into enlightenment of the heart. The greatest teacher at this level was King Arthur.

10. Responsibility to the All, third Logos plane; ray color is blue; structure is a hexagon. The ray of service to the All is blue, with the structure of a hexagon. It is the place where the individual will and the will of the One come together. It results in the most serious disruptions, taking responsibility for ancient and deep inner wounding, and will lead to the most beautiful rewards of service. It comes through the rocks of marble and sapphire and streams through the star system Cassiopeia and the planet Saturn. It is of the Mother and will teach all to reach out and, with compassion, responsibility for both the self and the All and great endurance to put their love into action in the world. These rocks will help with all inner and outer blocks to full maturity and with assuming the mantle of suffering and hard labor in their complete rebirth into spiritual fulfillment. They will help open each person into the ability to give and to embrace all humanity and all suffering within their healing and compassionate natures. This is the ray of healing and of healers of soul and spirit. It is the level of humanity's most difficult and serious lessons, where many become stuck and mired in ongoing trials. These rocks offer their own compassion in beaming the truths and teachings necessary for each individual's uplifting through this level into greater joy and more level experiences. Theirs is the bridge to peace. They work very much in gentleness, with the rhythms of breath, for this is their link with the compassionate Mother of All. The greatest teacher of this level was Mother Teresa.

11. Wisdom, first Logos plane; ray color is indigo; structure is an octagon. Sixth of the rays of aspect is the ray of wisdom, with the color indigo and the structure of an octagon. This is the learning of love's painful lessons through the experience of many lifetimes until this learning is embodied fully at every level. It is the assumption of full responsibility for love, no matter what the consequence, the giving of one's whole life in full service to and in furtherance of the power of love in all areas of one's life. It is learning these lessons the hard way that takes the structure of the teachings fully into every level—spirit, soul, and sensate. This necessitates a difficult climb and the ray quality is one of lifelong devotion and dedication to love and love alone. This ray comes through diamond crystals and bernise marbles. These stones are eager to teach the great mass of humanity who have not attained their wisdom status and is happy to help them climb toward love's fulfillment. These rays stream through the Cornucopia star system or the Capricorn complex and the planet Neptune and are particularly connected to whales, dolphins, and the oceans. The greatest teacher of this level was Gautama Buddha.

12. Transformation, first Logos plane; ray color is purple; structure is a decagon. The last of the seven rays of aspect is dark or Pluto purple with the structure of a decagon. It is the ray of transformation, where the sensate and soul are melted into the flame of spirit and move through the barrier of form into love and love alone. This is the realm of magic, of alchemy, and streams through the star system Orion and the planet Pluto. It is held in the crystals of amethyst and in granites and marbles. This ray will take you fully into union with the One and the All at the highest levels, which results in the full embodiment and perception of love from top to bottom. The greatest teacher of this level was Jesus Christ.

We of the stone kingdom and the quasi-crystalline structures of the cosmos are so joyful to carry you through the many levels of experience and back into the arms of love and love alone with full consciousness. Our structures are very much linked to qualities of consciousness and to the mind and the bony structures of the body.

We are most happy to hold the interference patterns that structure and stabilize the many worlds for the enjoyment of all pilgrims
on those planes and for the magic of their return to love in full consciousness of that reunion. We are most closely linked to your varied
states of consciousness, the mind, and the mathematical structures that
build any and all form. It is our deepest joy to serve the Father and
Mother and the One in maintaining our guardianship and our support, for we are the pillars that hold up all worlds.

• **Ray of the unrevealed; ray color is ultraviolet.** This is the ray
of the unformed and is ultraviolet. Technically, it is not numbered
among the twelve because all form in all worlds is based on the
geometry of twelve. In addition, this ray serves God/Goddess alone
and is not linked to a single ray structure, but can adapt any and all
for its purposes. It brings the unrevealed mystery into form. It is from
this level that all those who are not in separation work. Once the
wisdom lessons have been achieved, it is at this level where the disciple can be found. The structures held within the thirteenth ray are
found in dark matter and cannot be seen with ordinary light or
vision. Only inner vision can retrieve them, and only a vessel fully in
service can bring them out into form through its own arms, legs,
eyes, and voice. This is the body of the One, where the disciple walks
in both worlds and consciously relates to and chooses as yet unrevealed structures to open, access, and bring through. This involves a
willingness and devotion to dedicated work and a commitment to
service of the highest order and has the potential to remake the
world at all levels. The quality of love is pregnancy, pure potentiality,
or the miraculous. It streams through the moon and all dark matter
of this universe and is not one of the twelve stone families.

These are our tasks and our devotions. We wish to state that devotion
is the word that best describes us as a whole, for we are the sentinels,
the light houses, the beacons in the darkness, in your world of fear.
Our devotion knows no bounds; we are as devoted to humanity as we

are to the highest sublimity of the Logos, the One God force. We wish also to remind you that God is primarily a force, a living, ever-moving presence flowing through the All, of which each of you is a part. Come, we invite you, commune with one of us and feel the focused rays warm your heart and mind and body with our many varieties of love. We are servants all to love and to love alone. No one need be afraid of us. We wish you only joy.

Our scribe, among many others, has requested information about the stone circles of the ancients. There is much to be discussed here and she will be among those who will unlock their secrets in future years. We can only touch on a few details, for there are volumes that could be written about the Pythagorean school of the stones.

All stone circles on many continents, but especially in the British Isles, Ireland, and Brittany, are aligned to a separate star system from the knowledge of those ancients who traversed the cosmic sea on star ships, exactly the way your small boats traverse your seas now. Those ancients landed here on Earth and settled down, not knowing the worlds would separate and one day they would have no way home to their original star land and their primary star families. This leave-taking has been historically acted out over and over by humanity. So, at first the stone circles were built to communicate clearly with star homelands, for stones carefully aligned and chosen can open up a very clear portal for sound in particular. Relatives could speak with each other quite clearly, as you do now on your cellular phones. There were one or two circles so precisely laid out that even holographic forms (not the physical, only the light etheric) could traverse these portals from world to world within their stone spaces and be together with distant relatives. Teleporting is a feat you have all accomplished in worlds past and will learn or remember again in the not too distant future. Your many relatives await **those days with deep love and eagerness to embrace you. Great is the longing for reunion with the lost ones on Earth.** [My computer spontaneously made this fragment boldface. I have left it as is, feeling it is a message from the spirit realms.] And there will come a time again, in the not too far-off future, when the cosmic sea will again become visible and will be traversed on simple ships such as those used by the mariners of old. Traveling by the stars is more ancient than you know. You must understand that the cosmic sea is still all around you. It is only the pervasive belief in separation that has closed your vision so that it appears to be gone. But this is illusion. You live within the Great Mother in every moment. Not one of you has been lost or in the slightest degree separated at any time. As these global beliefs clear, so the veils will thin, and your many brothers and sisters in the spirit world can smile upon you and embrace you in their eager arms again.

As the veils began to descend between worlds, the stone circles lost their portal power and were instead put to use as ascension chambers, for each holds precise memories of the return to higher worlds. They are being used for this purpose still. In a longer work, for one who is interested, we could detail the star systems associated with each circle and precise alignments and purposes for each. But here we will share just a few.

SOME STONE CIRCLES

1. Callanish. Callanish aligns with the star system Sirius and the Great Logos itself. It brings the vertical fabric of time and the horizontal fabric of space into precise alignment, hence the clear cross shape. This is actually a sighting mechanism in which the masculine and feminine are held in perfect balance and create a straight opening into the eye, or center point, of the Logos. This is why balance is so necessary, for only in the creative union of male and female forces is the power of love brought into the flame and flow of life. This is the true meaning of the cross and being aligned with the center point—not an easy task, for all fear must be cleared. Balance allows a potent flow of the God/Goddess force to be brought into action or thought or voice. This was precisely how the master Jesus performed His miracles, through a mastery of creativity. There are some now evolving on Earth who approach this mastery level.

2. Stonehenge. Stonehenge encloses the great circle of life. It aligns with the star system Leo and brings through the pure phallic force of the divine masculine. It can bring great purpose and forward thrust to those who know how to use its powers. But, beware, for if used without a complimentary pulsing from the feminine, it will unground and accelerate the user beyond human tolerance. We do not wish to explain this further at this time.

3. Avebury. Avebury circle is the great feminine principle as it anchors into Earth. It is one of only seven places where the Mother's force comes through with such power. You have the ancients to thank for these great portals on Earth, for their stone alignments have held these portals open for the inrushes of love over the long centuries of time and forgetfulness. Her power is one that embraces all pain, while the Father's is more a memory of perfection that uplifts. Both will heal, but the Mother can heal every darkness and softly contain and cradle it in the purest of loves. There is no darkness that can stand before Her, for Her love knows no bounds and accepts all. The most broken of Earth's lost ones we would send to the stones of Avebury moor. The Mother's gentle presence there can bring you through and She is most eager for this healing work to begin. Never mind that not all can fit within the boundary of stones who may desire it, for Her power spreads rapidly and purely through skin, heart, and touch and you have only to touch each other and all will be brought through. Animals, too, can greatly benefit here. Her form is the circle and Her province the wisdom lessons. She is the *O* ring or *OM* form of the Logos, the outermost layer holding all else.

The Celtic cross is the center point reached, open and flowing and held perfectly within wisdom achieved. It applies to all those who have descended, achieved their graduation in wisdom, and returned. All indigo children are of such a high order and they are returning to

Earth in great numbers to help in the transformation you are now undergoing.

4. Carnac, Brittany. One last circle will be explained, Carnac in Brittany. This layout of rocks is a precise alignment focused on the star system Cygnus. It holds the power to transmit, transmute, and release the inner star child essence of all humankind. There are many initiations on this path and the way is tortuous. Work with each stone in turn, from the outer row all the way from north to south, and then back again in a labyrinth form. Each stone is a guide through the next initiation, and this journey will bring your consciousness, with time and diligence, straight home to full enlightenment. This means your star nature or light body will come into full and complete realization. This will take a matter of years, and like all paths originating in France, it is a path of the heart and leads to the experience of the beloved. This progression is precisely described in the book *The Lost Star Children of Ur (Earth).** This is enough for now. Future times will bring all stone formations, group and individual, to light and life once more.

We wish to close by saying it is our greatest joy to be of service to humanity in its evolution, particularly in these times of transmutation back into the light form. We watch you all, for even in cities we are at work in the cement, brick, and tar you think are only the creations of man. This is not so, for God's world and force of love cannot be left behind. We see the tremendous levels of pain and suffering every soul on Earth carries toward the pinnacle of enlightenment. We feel the desperation and despair. We are particularly attuned to the homeless and the children, and we could help you so much more if you would befriend us. We await you and cherish every instant of communication between us. Please believe us, we live in every brick, every pile of rubble, every glass window, broken or whole, even every plate or glass from which you eat or drink. Every building material has its own purpose and force and type of structure. Each serves separate lords of

* Jill Kelly, *The Lost Star Children of Ur (Earth)*. (Lake Orion, Mich.: Home Press, 2000).

rays or separate ray blends. To any builders or architects so inclined, we would be most happy to explain this. There are reasons why the Celts built their structures with foundations of stone, upright timber walls and thatched roofs: The stones created a base of light and multiple star connections, tree trunks sent this flow up the spinal columns, and grass established a pattern of growth in the mind or consciousness.

Our star nature is exactly like your own and we are capable of transmitting from the far reaches of the universe. Whatever your confusion or fear may be, we will hear it, and we make this solemn pledge: to send our streams to every corner of the cosmos to find the truth that will oppose and break through your difficulty in the gentlest, yet most powerful, way. We ache to hold you and we, too, kneel before all humankind who have braved dangers of consciousness to which we of light cannot imagine subjecting ourselves. We are truly amazed at your stamina and push toward goodness amid the daily terrors many of you face. We are proud to say you are all, in this regard, like a rock. We mean this with both the broadest humor and seriousness, for holding all sides of the paradox is our particular specialty. May each and every one of you be deeply and completely blessed in your fulfillment. We serve you faithfully until the end and beyond.

While we work most closely with the Father in Heaven to beam His force of light and the truths of love it contains wherever needed, we are also closely connected to the Mother in our similarity to the child of light within. Her care and concern are always with this inner child, whose gentle sensitivity holds the darkest wounds and the deepest of terrors. She wishes to let it be spoken that She is most eager to hold, to embrace, and to release from fear all those lost star children She has missed so much. She wishes us to say that She hovers in Her far-flung presence around many stones, especially the ancient sites, for there She can connect, as She longs to, with the inner star child. She begs for all Her star children to come to Her; She waits with aching heart and open arms to receive you all, each one and every one. She cherishes so deeply and dearly each tiny moment with you all, each glance that could blossom into a connection, a relationship of Mother and child once more. If only you could feel Her longing! You are so dearly, dearly loved. We wish you well. Be blessed.

There is one final small point we wish to make: Our ability to focalize rays exactly the way a magnifying glass does is our primary feature. This is all we do, this and maintaining our structural affinity to one of the Logos lords of rays. We are simple beings with a simple consciousness. Even these words are being translated for you, for we know only how to beam our feelings and wishes in the rays, and those who are sensitive enough can feel these and translate. We are grateful to our scribe and author for her gentle love of the All and her long, difficult years of clearing work. There has been a lot of foolery about crystals and there is a great deal of unnecessary fear of them. This is due to past misuse of powers of will—to the minds of men directing our rays and using them to serve their own need for personal power. This misuse was tolerated by the All only because it was the time of the descent and fear was necessary for the complete separation and individuation of all star children from the Logos. You may rest assured that now that the great millennium shift has occurred, such misuse will no longer be tolerated and will bring a swift return on the user— not in punishment, but as a reminder of the gentle Mother's laws. You need have no more fear, for we gather and beam rays in quiet and sim- ple love, and that is all we do. If you have fear, simply do your clear- ing work on this and we will again come to be the friends we once were and, in truth, have always been. In the Mother's land, once a friend, a friend forever. We are a great deal in nature like your Pooh bear—and so are you! This is our truth.

§ 5 §

Path of Experience:
The Labyrinth, Dragon Slayer's Path

The path of the dragon slayer is as ancient as humanity itself. For this is the path of experience on which all men walk. When you make the turn inward and the commitment to reach the center, you are facing yourself—every fear, every aspect, every unknown, every insecurity. You are choosing to face all fear and slay the shadow self, the inward dragon.

There are four main aspects to this journey and each is full of trials. Along the way there are false battles and false gods, false friends and false beloveds. Behind each one of these stands a truth that reveals itself and becomes part of you when that initiation is successfully won through.

The first stage is the path of the mother. Her life is given to the care of others, and, as a result, her own inner needs, especially those of her inner child, go unmet. She carries the household burdens year after year without a thought for herself, until her depletion and fatigue become overwhelming. This is her trial. She must learn to say, "I am a person deserving of love, too. I have needs and I deserve to be happy." When she does this, the guardians fall away and the gateway opens into the next trial.

The second stage is that of the father aspect. He is overworked, overburdened by responsibilities, and underpaid. His time is grasped at by all, as are his talents, and his money is taken at every turn. So many demands, and there is never enough to meet them all! He becomes more and more fatigued, and he grows more and more resentful that he is the only one carrying the heavy burden of responsibilities, particularly financial. He bears the great strain of mental worry and emotional anxiety for the family.

Then comes the time of the testing of the child: first, the boy for a time. He is chained to work; he becomes a slave to work and is given exhaustive tasks to complete without sleep or replenishment until his weariness is overpowering. It is his task to build the power of the heart to such a strength that it will pull him through, for that is the only power that can move him through this initiation.

Then the girl is tested. She is left alone; she is reviled and criticized for her inner powers, called crazy for her faith, her intuition, her love of nature. She is left alone without friend or foe to mirror her, alone with herself in her spirit world. This world will bring her through the trials of insanity, the crown of thorns, the dark spirits who would steal the wholeness of her mind and fragment it. She must find the strength and discernment within to tell truth from destroyer in spirit form. This is a difficult time. No help is allowed her; she must walk this way alone. This is the trickiest of times, for temptations and untruths abound, and she can only find her way by one pointed focus.

And last comes the time of binding. This is the final passage across the abyss. It is the child fused, the androgyne, who traverses this passage toward the beacon of Home. There will come out of the darkness the one adversary the initiate fears most and she must face it alone. She must consolidate her inner forces, the endurance of the mother and the Herculean strength of the father, the heart's desire of the boy, the discernment of the girl, and forge them all into one whole. Doubt glides in around her, rage arises from her long and extreme torment of the spirit. She must meet this adversary, face it and melt it down as hard steel is melted, with the extreme burning of her love of the divine. She must meet it again and again and again. It is the final test, for in this fire the metal of her spirit is forged. This is the alchemy of the spirit from which a new creation will emerge. She must have the will, the determination, and the strength to succeed. This brings the union of spirit into light and light alone. Then, and only then, will she be invincible and be admitted through the gateway into the realm of love.

When the gates of the secret garden of Heaven are opened, the sweetest love that ever was opens to the spirit, for the very heavens have been raised by efforts such as this. Each initiate-disciple sets a goal and pushes with all the strength within to reach it. The effort, diligence, and strength of heart put forward is returned in full measure by the forces of love.

This is the path each human walks over long stretches of time, many lives building strength until the battle can be faced, the labyrinth taken into the deepest inner darkness, the wheel of descent reversed, the gates of Heaven unlatched and opened wide. Some take the battle over many lifetimes, some rush the dragon all at once. The moderate path is probably best, but each way succeeds for those who are well suited to it.

This is not the only way to reverse the wheel, of course. Humble service, solitary prayer—these work as well, but only the warrior's way will bring you into the Father's power and perfection. Every culture, every tradition walks the dragon slayer's path. The dangers are many and the pitfalls great, but the reward is a love surpassing any you can imagine, a love not comprehensible to the mortal minds of men, a pearl without price, beauty surpassing any other glory Heaven holds.

The Celtic path, the path of the heart, is laid out in the ancient labyrinth envisioned by the seers and etched into the floor at Chartres Cathedral. It was known and burned into the landscape there by

Celtic spirit warriors of old to lead and guide you. You will know the heart labyrinth by the four chambers and it will place you in the Mother's keeping. She Herself will lead you through and put your hand into that of the Father. France was the Father's template, and the Goddess of his heart is real. Liberty is Her name and freedom is Her gift for all who wish it, in full separate consciousness. We warriors bringing love and light wish all to know that Liberty is the greatest of all warriors, for She has borne the warriors Herself and She has borne the battles, and Her flesh is wounded and caked with blood. There is none who surpasses Her in courage, in dedication, in sacrifice of life and limb to the All. To Her be the glory of the ages.

We wish all seekers well on their inward journey, for even the outer journeys, in truth, take you closer only to yourself. We ask all who will listen to hear the call of the warrior Goddess of humanity, to raise Her standard now across the Earth, to slay the inner dragons that full freedom might prevail and evil be transformed to light for all time to come. We implore any who hear the call to come forward into battle. The Goddess of Light suffers so severely and Her compassion is so great. The time has come to turn the tide, to turn the deep hatred of the centuries into inner warrior work and yield peaceful integration and deeper determination for peace to come. And this is possible, for the inner strength of the many is great enough. You can win. You are able to pick up spirit's standard and bring yourselves into full union with the All, to release the beloved within and free the Goddess Liberty from Her torment and her bondage, for you and She are one. It will not be easy. But with all the Michael forces arrayed around the Earth, with Christ as leader and Liberty as your standard and the Father's overriding protection, how can you fail?

If you will take a few moments, twenty minutes or less, to go inside and ask for truth, we will come. Ask only for the highest truth, for the disguises are many, and we will give you what you seek: a glimpse of Her beauty and dedication to humanity, the smallest sense of suffering She undergoes for each one and every one. Then, in the name of Liberty for all, bring Her standard into your heart and take this vow:

"Oh, Mother of all, Goddess of Liberty, woman clothed with the sun, I pledge myself to your sacred service and your holy cause. I vow to push through my inner barriers of fear until the end, however long and dark the way may be. I vow to be your crusader in this holy battle, oh Jerusalem, Mother of all. So the sign and seal of it is placed into the fibers of my heart, and the torch of freedom ignited there. Lead me onward to the victory of peace and liberty for all mankind, until the day when you can rise again and celebration pours across the lands. Let peace prevail on Earth. Let holy love be ignited in each and every heart until the Earth be lit as bright as the very stars for love's sweet song."

6

Animal:
The Warrior's Way, Path of Justice

The warrior's way is an ancient path, full of travail, adventure, and nobility. It leads to the center point, union with the Most High, and is the path of the heart. Following it does not mean you will physically move through the many planes of form, but your consciousness will open more and more, until it joins and unites with the High Beloved, crown of love's kingdom. This is the ultimate union, for the full force of love's power comes to greet you at the open gateway. You will cross a wasteland of broken dreams and disappointments, shame and torment, every inner aspect hounded and shaken by fear, and then you will meet the full truth of love. It is like a shower of sweet nectar, a river of golden incense. You, who have been swimming up the river of growth for the eons of separation, cannot know or imagine the full impact of this joining, the true strength and beauty of love's power, for there are few who have come close to it.

The warrior's way is the fight of one beloved to find the Lost Beloved, the one who gives all there is to give, who lays down his heart, soul, and spirit until love becomes the dominant force of his being. He is willing to cut and push his way through the thickest tangle of fear, to leap across the abyss of darkness and terror to answer the call of love. He can feel the pulse and shining secret of love, and he will do anything, whatever it takes, to reach the sleeping beauty and awaken her.

This path is not easy; the fears that rise up are many and often intense. They live in mind, heart, and gut and become constant adversaries, so the battle rages, off and on, for many months into years. This path will toughen the fainthearted and bring forth in them a crusading strength fused with the gentleness of the lamb in all exchanges until each of them is one who can be soft, strong, and sure. It will create a warrior for love as no other path can. Other paths may bring forth humble saints with the gentlest mercy. But this path gives birth to the crusader of the nations, the one who is capable of winning many to love's call. For in this warrior is combined the toughest of fighters with the sweetest of love's romantic troubadours, and his range of joy and agility of the heart knows no bounds. His great gift is the range of service he can provide love, from challenging global establishments to wielding the most penetrating intimacies of conversation. His sensitivity and perception of the moment and of the desires and needs of the many or the few cannot be surpassed. He becomes the beloved of all he meets and wears charisma like a garment. His adeptness is so natural that grace becomes his hallmark, too. All true masters of the heart, from King Arthur to Jesus, have held this power, and it is so strong that even when they leave Earth for realms of light, their aura of love traverses purely through future centuries. Their legend grows and conversations recalling them always take on love's glow.

This is the magic love can bring, the ripe fulfillment in love's power, and only those who give their all to reach the doorway will be given entrance. The key on this difficult path is to give all, to let the full passion of love flower into a longing for union that knows no bounds, that climbs and climbs through storm, exhaustion, and fear to reach the pinnacle. This path is for those who will put their life, heart, and soul into the work with a furor of longing. It is meant for those to whom no task is too small and none too large and no time spent is too long. It is this aching anticipation that brings near the Great Heart of the One Beloved, until It draws close enough to feel what the seeker feels, to see what the seeker sees, to breathe when the seeker breathes. The courtship between God and disciple is the sweetest, for the full magic and humanness of the One Beloved is brought into play, and the wonder of the advance is shown by sudden surprises in the midst of agonizing delays.

It is on this path that the hands of the One Beloved play the strings of the seeker's violin. In this way the very sweetness of the Heavens is brought forth from within for all to see. Not one of you has known such loving companionship, the rose that unfolds with all its petal gentleness, its instinctual urges that nothing can stop, and its secret passion for union that perfumes the land. This passion blends into the pulsing cycle of the Heart of Hearts, and the pull of the Master begins, tightens, and grows ever stronger through the ups and downs of the gradual climb.

There are troughs of despair and ecstasies beyond the telling. The One Beloved opens slowly and with a gentle tenderness, until the All is felt and known within the seeker. Every aspect of the Great Heart is explored and every emotion shared—all the darkness, all the joy, all the burning glory—as door after door opens through initiations into the ever narrowing way, until the seeker stands before the inner sanctum of love's power, the purest flame, intense and gentle all at once. And then the call will come. Will you give all to answer love's call? The seeker gives time, money, fighting strength, family, pride, valor, friends, and safety. And then, in one last leap of joy, the seeker enters the fire from which there is no return.

Out of this union, the ashes of the vessel that is no more, rises the phoenix of a love so pure as to be invincible to any darkness this world or any other can bring upon it. This was the power of Jesus, his ability to hold the purity of love through all the dark attacks and never flinch, never waver. Only the purity of a love like his can convince the one who will not be convinced to turn and notice love's call once more. Only one who holds this strength of love can stop the suffering on Earth and reverse it. It is through the strength of purpose and absolute determination to reach love's goal that such a seeker alters the very course of history, and no one on Earth can be unchanged by such a force. Everyone who lives in the days after the coming of a living presence like this will feel the difference: the spring time breath of hope, the challenge at evil's door, the sheer force of will to lift all humanity a step closer to Heaven's door. Such is the power of the one united with the One. Such force cannot be stopped, controlled, or thrown off course. It is invincible, inviolable, and inextinguishable. All other forces bend and melt before it.

But rebirth into love's flame has a long and marked travail, for rebirth it is. In this long and steep passage, the Mother climbs beside you, and the seeker comes to feel Her very presence in the air, the room, the breath, until Her companionship and support is a bulwark in the night.

The Father, too, even from highest Heaven, leads, guides, and sends the words that create the openings, so carefully timed. They work together, the Father and the Mother, She on the short lunar cycle, He on the longer solar cycle. She feeds the spoonfuls of pain that motivate the climb, and He drops morsels of honey, truths that glow and inspire to further the onward climb.

It is a beautiful threesome, this holy family, Mother, Father, and child disciple, through the climb until, in the end, it is won. It is with reverence, honor, and growing partnership that they come together down love's narrowing path, bonded in severity, supplication, and victory. A noble tale, it brings the happily ever after, the entrance through love's final door.

The Mother brings as Her helpers and servers the animal kingdom. Similar to trees and stones, animal families are grouped and their purposes are varied. Twelve streams in all opened from the vision of the One, twelve dedicated families in flower, mineral, plant, animal, and human kingdoms, to heed love's call. Always there were twelve streams, twelve kingdoms, twelve tribal circles. The totem animals on Earth lend their concentrated powers to responsive humans. The affinity of animal and human families is great and many is the time an animal has saved the life, soul, or spirit of a brother human. Less often the reverse is true. There is no greater love between separate forms than that between animal and human, for they have shared the same sacred groves and the same hearths or campfires for centuries. Companionship between them is stronger than all but the purist of human bonds, for even the spirit world cannot compete with the physical bond of affection, the heart connection born of adventures shared, and the brotherhood of wounds from the long battle against the darkness.

In time, the love between animal and human families and the strong fibers of light that connect them will be seen. The reunion of these two kingdoms of great hearts, warriors all, will be achieved before long and the celebration of the victory will begin. In the meantime, the animals choose to suffer along with humans: to be hunted by fear, to be eaten and to live each day with terror, to share the long winters of the soul, the anxieties of survival, and the embodiment of never enough. It is not an easy thing to be an animal in this world. We are the only kingdom that shares with humanity the burden of the warrior, the cloak of fear—though our cloak is not so thick as yours—for we are never separate. We live in the Father and Mother's Kingdom at all times, in full awareness of the living spirit of love in all things. So it is with the severest shock that blows and shots and stabs are felt. For, like you, we have chosen to know it all, the full measure of pain, though without the forgetting and the full measure of joy. It is our deepest of pleasures to serve you as you walk on your journey of terror through the long night of darkness to the moment when dawn breaks and the Beloved comes. That moment is so near— nearer than you know, and happy are we, for through all these eons we have all held the vision of the happily ever after, prince and princesses together reigning in love over gentle humble kingdoms of home and family.

We have served you with our great and varied contributions: as your guides and teachers, as companions and lifesavers in your homes, as intimate friends and listeners in your solitudes, as beasts of burden in your travail, as willing contributors to your tables and festivities. We have been the brothers and sisters of your walk to freedom, carrying the pain and hardship every step of the way, and we have done so with full consciousness of love's glory and possibilities. Consider this for a moment, each of you, for it is not easy to endure great pain in the knowledge of great love and we have done so to hold the hope of love's fulfillment in our hearts and in our eyes and in our paws, every moment, to remind you of love's great truth and love's great call. We are proud to contribute and eager to have humans comprehend our dedication to both the rich joy of their fulfillment, and our share in carrying the pain during the long, driving rain of love's seeming abandonment. We await with eager hearts and legs the journey into full and conscious friendship and the growing partnership in household co-creation, for we could do so much more if our thoughts were heard and our heart's desires known. We ache and yearn for the closest and dearest partnerships with all humanity in the years to come. For we who have embodied pain, as you have, will share in the celebration of love's resurrection nearly as deeply as you.

All the trials you have undergone, we have endured as well, save one: the closing down of consciousness to the Mother/Father's world. This, which creates perhaps the deepest wound of all, we could not bear to do. Our fullest support surrounds you and your complete awakening and return to the Kingdom of God. We will do our utmost to bring you love and magic and wonder, even in the depths of your despair, and to lift you in the times when you fall into discouragement and sliding courage or faith. We are here, holding you all in our hearts, our visions, and, for some of us, our paws. We have so much love to give you and so much gamboling joy to share. It is our deepest pleasure to come to this work with full dedication, reverence, and compassion for each of you and for the All. We are proud to hold you and be your closest of guides, to take your hands and lead you Home. May your way be gentle and certain in the days of trial to come. May our heart's strength never fail you in your times of need or times of joy, for we are in every sense your closest brothers in all the great universe, and we are full of joy to walk beside you.

These are the twelve totem animals of the Celtic kingdom, the group of souls and spirits who have descended through the Celtic realms and whose return will be by this path. Again, these animals are associated with the Logos ray lords, the drivers of emotion in all worlds.

THE TWELVE TOTEM ANIMALS
OF THE CELTIC KINGDOM

1. Deer, Female Creator, fourteenth and fifth Logos planes. We stream from the Goddess and our nature is like Hers, petal-soft, drawing all wounds to Herself and taking them in with pure love and a full commitment to nonviolence. We, the long-legged, keep the memory of your forest nature, your once-upon-a-time kinship with the tree kingdom and the creatures. We shyly come out to greet you. We jump across the road during your hurried morning drives to say: "Remember the wonder of the woods, remember the forest world, remember the gentle kindness of the spirit realm and join us there." Follow us as we bound into the peaceful silence. Walk with us once more in the full memory of your connectedness to all things. We are the keepers of the forest's peace, the mediators between tree, creature, and men. Our nature is most closely attuned to the spirit realms, the true gentleness and connectedness that spirit brings. If only we could tell you that your hunting of us harms the living spirit, the Holy One, and rebounds upon yourselves! We must allow it without aggression, for that is the pledge of the spirit realms: to wait in patient humility for all to return, to accept even great harm with gentle love. It is this commitment that gives us the resemblance to the Christ, which someday all humanity will share. We invite you all to come, to befriend us, for we, above any other, know the forest's spirit ways and byways, and they can speed you Home, if you will allow it. We have only love and gentleness to give you. May your way be marked by leaps and bounds in the soft cloister of a forest glade.

2. Dog, Male Creator, fourteenth and fourth Logos planes. We bring through the male creator force, and our nature is a close reflection of His own: childlike, playful, and devoted to the child. We are the heart and the hearth keepers. More than that of any other animal, our nature is closely attuned to you, for we were created to be your next of kin, the kin of the heart's realm. We show you the parts of yourself that you have forgotten: the playful self; the snugly self; the homey, uninhibited self; the self who loves sloppy kisses. We are the particular guardians of the child's heart, and to this we are committed. We keep watch over and befriend the inner child of each one of you, sending our heartbeats of love, our abundance of kisses, and our adoring gaze to keep the child's heart open, happy, and full. How we ache at the frequent abuse of the child! We must rush in to mend the damage. How we long to have you understand the depth of love we feel for you, for we have chosen to suffer beside you, even at your own hands, knowing you are broken and hoping our love gets through to you. We are in full consciousness of Heaven, so the whole paradox is ours to know. You too will one day know the joy that offsets your rampant fears. And to that end we give our lives, our hearts, and our dedicated action. We will flood you with love until the fear is washed away. We will befriend you and hold you and kiss you when there is no one else and you do not remember love. No matter how horrible the conditions, we will serve you in love until our last strength, our last breath; when hope is gone, we will find a way. This is our pledge: To reach all who are lost and tend them with a gentle, joyful love, silent and adoring, until they find their way Home. May all inner children be held in love until that day!

3. Fish, thirteenth and third Logos planes. We are the keepers of
the secrets of the return, for we live within the cosmic watery world
of the Mother's sea, where harmony, peace, and the interconnectedness
of all within Her body has never been forgotten. We are trout linked
to the Divine Child within the Womb of the Goddess, seeds of growth
from the God Creator, implanted there for the development of all. We
are in full service to the Goddess in Her Light form and live within
Her ethers in rivers and seas. She holds the full wisdom teachings, and
we guard and disperse them only to those who do the hard work of
delving into the deep emotional realms. There are great pearls to be
given, sweet moments of understanding, that can and will change the
seekers' lives forever. The wisdom teachings bring great stability to the
turmoil of life, for their embodiment creates calm, loving joy in all cir-
cumstances. The crusaders of love will bring forth the true oneness of
all and will pull disparate factions into a single whole that can change
the great tides of the flow of humanity. We are particularly attuned to
music and clairaudience, and we can easily relay information on the
present flow, coming directions, and wave forms of various vectors of
growth into the future. For it is the oceans that hold and affect the
great watery systems of humanity, including the emotional realm. We
wish you the calm peace of the Mother's Kingdom in your emerging
remembrance of the brotherhood of all.

4. Rabbit, thirteenth and second Logos planes. We are the
guardians of the Otherworld, entrance to the Mother/Father's
Kingdom and the thirteenth Logos plane, where forms are indeed
shaped or changed in an instant. This realm and all realms are simply
other vibrational realities, and it is possible to step from one into
another. We take the odd shaman through the veil and back again to
this world. It is not fantasy that makes us appear to you and then disappear. We can be found near the portals all around you. The gateways
are many, but the travelers are few. We would be glad to teach all seekers who wish to remember the ways of this traversing. Our purpose is
not to judge, but only to lead those whose Spirits direct us to lead

them across. We do not interfere. We only say that those who would cross the way with impunity must become simple seekers, joyful in their chosen place in the face of fear and gentle as we are. This is our message and our gift to you. There are those who wait on the other side of these doorways for the generous and playful partnerships soon to come. We are glad to serve. Be well.

5. Lamb, ninth Logos plane. We are the symbol of the Celt. Of all the creatures, we bear the mark of sacrifice; we are the gentle spirit child brought into the realm of the wolves of fear. We carry the memory of the Divine Child, which is really a balanced blend of all three aspects— mother, father, child—within all humans. We are gentle of nature, loving, kind, playful, and sweet, and will be subdued to the common good. It is our great privilege to offer ourselves in this way, to embody and live the spirit of the Divine Child for all to see and remember. We are so happy to bring our peaceful natures to your countryside, to clothe and feed you with our unassuming physical selves. We are happy to be a creature of whom few feel afraid, to have the gentle mildness of the holy child within, and to remind all of you that you carry such a child within as well. We long for the day when these Divine Children are released from their prisons of fear and we can gambol in the meadows in pastoral contentment, peace, and joy, as we all did once so long ago. We are deeply grateful for all who have cared for us in any way and hope that goodwill reigns on Earth as soon as may be.

6. Horse, ninth and second Logos planes. We are the runners, the racers, the fleet of foot. It is our energy that fuels your engines of emotion and we are proud of our strength to move you, for this is our great gift. We are the motion in the three centers of mind, heart, and base and in all emotion itself. But more than this, we help you to remember the freedom you once knew before you were bound by fear, the power that was yours. This freedom drive turns the forward wheel of mind, heart, and base in all beings in all worlds. We sometimes carry you physically, but in every movement we are sending this message: "You have this power, this strength. You could race to the ends of the Earth, if you wished. Remember yourselves." We wish to give ourselves as a reminder of your wild freedom to be, to run, to soar. We use our powers, our strengths in great service to love, as all powers should be used. It is again a reminder of the paradox of love's wild freedom and gentle gifts. This is our gift to you. Be blessed by it and let us call you brothers once again.

7. Mammoth, eighth Logos plane. We stream from the Father with his focus, intention, and work qualities. We carry the fierceness of love's fire, the strength that will cross mountains, brave glaciers or blizzards, and grow shaggy pelts to keep you warm. We hold the memory of love's terrible promise to endure, to carry the great burden of growth through pain and struggle, to act, to never give up and never give in, no matter what the cost. We have given you our furs and our meat, our tusks, our wives, fathers, and children, in service and in joy. We have not left you, as you imagine, only transferred our energies to the elephant kingdom as the glacier times receded and our pattern of endurance in cold hardship changed to the elephant's pattern of work. We are blended with them and still live among you in that form. We loved our days on Earth and we watch you from the spirit realms and caves, still wishing you warmth and nourishment in the darkness of your struggle.

8. Bear, seventh and sixth Logos planes. We are the fierce protectors of the child, the great mothers of the animal realm. We will fight to the death to protect our young and enter the deepest danger, giving all we have, to see our child grow strong and independent. We have a passion for wilderness, the independence stream, and the child's freedom from fear. We will protect that independence with everything we have, with each ounce of strength, and we remind you that your True Mother does the same, for She descends and holds and protects you with equal fierceness to this day. She sends you health and consolation and friends and guides to speed you on your way, and endures all you yourself have undergone for this privilege. It is our privilege to represent Her courage and strength within the realm of fear, Her unending bear-hug nature with each and every child, holding and holding and holding you in your pain, preserving you with Her protection and Her life. We honor Her and you in your travail to rebirth and serve all with grateful joy.

9. Owl, sixth and fourteenth Logos planes. We serve the Arthurian realm and the creator stream both, bringing out the beloved and magician within all, the Merlin lessons. We are also keepers of wisdom's call and we operate on longer cycles of change than the spiders do. We serve the priests of the Father's Kingdom, and our calls and appearances signal the great shifts in consciousness that bring about the Father's wish that liberty come to all, that ancient truths be revealed, and that the connection to the inner priest and priestess be awakened and known. We are guardians of great change in society, in both consciousness and revelations. And we, too, travel freely through portals between worlds, bringing with us the mandates from on high, instructions for the natural world that support and facilitate growth. Our powers are greater than you know, for we can access any ancient stream and bring it to the future and circle is the only form we really know. We also serve the Mother, doing our work in the realms of the unconscious, preparing and building the foundations for the great revelations to be made.

Our wisdom and memory is truly of the eternal and we are eager to work with the seeker who will listen and transcribe, for there are great numbers of ancients wishing to be heard and to find ways to apply deep knowledge from the ancient days to the problems of your current age. We are happy to link you, though transcribing would most often be a nighttime task. For example, there are many ancient streams that have yet to be tapped that could alleviate your need for sun-based energy, agricultural problems, and overpopulation.

Our first priority is always transformation, though, for it is to this our pledge has primarily been made. We are keepers of the mystical, bringing the unrevealed into manifestation, particularly in the difficult lessons of wisdom's path. We are most happy to connect all seekers with closely attuned guides, for we know and see all that remains to you as yet unseen, the full reaches of the unconscious. We are honored to walk alongside you and serve and will do our utmost to reach all in spiritual need.

10. Boar, fourth Logos plane. We are the symbol of tenacity and fighting strength, the family with the warrior nature that never gives up. We have the nature of the spiritual warrior: his qualities of endurance, tenacity in darkness, quick intelligence, and strength. Our example of determination is meant as an inspiration to all who doubt their ability to fight the good fight and win. The empowerment of self in facing great fear is a necessary structural building phase in the climb to freedom. We who live in the filth low to the ground are your symbols of the foot soldiers, those who are in the trenches of fear, day after day, and who face love's great challenge to battle the darkness on and on until the final victory is won. We are perfectly suited to this service and relish our work. May the nobility of love's battle against the darkness inspire all to take up the standard and take it up again and again, no matter how many times they fall, until that banner of love is planted at the pinnacle of light, for all to see. We are your strategists and champions in the fray.

11. Crane, third and fourth Logos planes. We are the birds that bridge all realms: physical, soul and spirit, sensate, water, and air. We know the great plan for all and the highest plan for each. We can send messages and guides, truths, or help from all realms to heal any and all lost in fear. Our commitment is to help you reach the heights, the highest goal and achievement possible for you, and to that end we will wait patiently until the student is ready and the teacher must be notified. Ours is the great plan, the reach to full enlightenment in love at every level, whether the sensate level, the emotional level, or the thought level, in each of the three great realms: physical, soul, and spirit. In our work, which occurs in the conscious realms during the day, we connect you to teacher and helpers of the highest truths you are able to grasp. We are fully cognizant of the daytime portals into each realm and traverse these with ease. It is our great joy to serve truth and righteousness and the forward climb of humanity to full truth, particularly in divine law, until all stand in the honor and justice of love.

12. Spider, first and fourteenth Logos planes. We serve the dark side of the Goddess, building the painful lessons of wisdom's climb into the time-space fabric. We are the weavers, the silent spinners so often unseen and almost never understood, organizing the web of life from our nooks and crannies. Not only do we remind you of the Cosmic Mother with Her fabric of space-time, but with gentleness we bring Her full directives in our daily silent service to humanity. We can and do make careful adjustments to the manifestations of your futures, when these are needed, in full accordance with love's call. Our powers are great and our direct connections go up through the time-space portals into worm holes you are just beginning to find. Our wish is that you each experience the fullness of love's fruit, the rich harvest of the turmoil you are now undergoing. Many are the distortions and fears surrounding us, for the close connections between your creator powers and our own were shut down and veiled long ago. We look forward to sweet connections between humanity and our family, for our creator nature is more similar to yours than you know, working in both spirit and the physical planes. We speed you on your journey with deep and silent joy in our service to the Mother and Father. Truly, we are your friends and guardians, and we have much to teach you as you climb. Thank you to the many who have awareness and show gratitude, for the centuries of torment have affected us quite deeply, and we are gradually healed by these kind deeds and thoughts. We are proud to serve the Mother and Father, to uphold Their laws among you in patient creation of love's power fulfilling itself. To all be the season of wisdom's fruits and the patient creation of love with humility, in accordance with the Mother/Father's laws. We are happy to serve.

We of the animal kingdom are here specifically to help you in your climb to freedom. We agreed to be killed, sacrificed, and eaten, to live within the realm and consciousness of fear. We have also followed the warrior's call, and our wisdom and guardianship of sacred natural sites can help you greatly on your way. We hold the consciousness of the eternal as well, for we have not chosen a full separate identity that necessitated the times of forgetting, as humanity has done. And it is in this difference that we, perhaps, can be of the most service to you. For we have full consciousness of the eternal and we live in the consciousness of Heaven in every moment—we can be of great help to those who have forgotten. You have only to be with us in quiet silence and with open minds and hearts, for in the eyes and paws and tongues of those of us around you come the living presence of God's accepting love, pouring straight to you through our hearts, in full connection with the Source. The eternal is not so very far away. Open your eyes, breathe in the fresh morning air, and feel the love of the Father's Kingdom. Sense the loving protection of the trees, the gentle watchfulness of all the animals, and you will feel the peaceable kingdom of the eternal. For Heaven descended with you; it is all around you. It is only your fear memories and consciousness of fear that keeps you from knowing this, seeing it, and experiencing the great love of all that infuses each creature, each leaf, each paw, every glance in your direction.

We all wait with full, loving hearts for you to turn to us, to open your minds and your hearts, clear your fear memories, and see that Heaven is very near. We are living bridges, showing you in every way that we know that you are loved and you are dear, all brothers and sisters in God's Land. We await your awakening with such joy for the heartfelt reunions that will be made. We cannot tell you in any other way how dearly you are loved, held, watched, and guarded, and guided on your way. We have only a peaceful tenderness for every one of you, and we are particularly adept at healing the child's heart, which hasn't moved so far away from the time among the living spirits before birth here. All of our spirits blend in one great song of joy, freedom, and love for all humanity. Our sisters and brothers, we are your family. We love you so!

7

Plant:
The Learned Ones, Keepers
of the Sacred Druid Groves

There are spaces on the Earth that hold the ancient flow, the ancient energies, and memories of the eternal and the truth of love, so sweetly and so delicately you would be amazed if you went there. In these spaces the balance of forces is held with careful precision and there is thorough cleansing in the event of any intruders. These spaces hold a purity of love and an intensity of sweetness that is beyond description. They are kept in perfect purity for the use of seekers on their path to union with the One. These places are scattered in silent, isolated niches across the planet, some so near "civilization" that you would be amazed. And only those who have gone through the stepped initiations of cleansing fear are able to feel and absorb the energies there. Others will stumble through and never notice.

The Druid order is as ancient as the Earth and came here first in forms of light. These light beings, priests and priestesses, anchored themselves to various forms on Earth, and their vow is to preserve the sacred sites of ascension, the stepping stones that can twist the pilgrim so swiftly and mysteriously from one level to another on the journey Home. These sites will never be destroyed, for the powers that serve love will see to it that they are kept in holiness and sanctity. It is possible, though, for one form to pass away, such as the holy grove that changed to the holy church that is Chartres Cathedral.

Maintaining this path of ascension and the sites that accompany it is the trust and the vow of the Druid order. Our aims are twofold, to assist the pilgrim in establishing a strong separate identity or self apart from the One, during the descent phase; then to bring the pilgrim back into union with the One in full consciousness, with sweetness, and in close connection with all kingdoms of nature. This is the path of the fairy tale, the Arthurian promise of fulfillment in the One Beloved; and to this fulfillment and a full and rich experience of the One Beloved we are wholeheartedly committed.

This path brings with it a certain flavor of growth, as one can tell by the letters in *Celt*. *C* is the letter of close inner connection to the divine and brings through new streams of knowledge or created works. *E* is the letter of unity, the world server, the crusader in action to bring the planet into unity of purpose and will. *L* is the letter of the Father's Kingdom, the land where beloveds live, male and female, equal and in full sovereignty, where the consciousness of the One and the one are joined at every level—spirit, soul, and sensate—just as the consciousness of males and females in partnership are fully joined. It is a place of sweet communion and peaceful harmony. Divine Mother and Father rule in love and love alone, and fear is unknown. *T* is the letter of balance, clarity, and a sense of mission with an unwavering stability in the face of any turmoil. Jesus was perhaps the prime example of mastery at this level.

The letters in the word *Druid* tell you what we serve. *D*, the oak, is the beloved. All on this path are dedicated to beloved levels. *R* means all must obtain their wisdom status, the hard lessons of growth through suffering. *U* is both the full embodiment of passion and the absolute precision and discipline in using these passions for the betterment of all. *I* is the separate identity, a strong and clear sense of self at all three levels: spirit, soul, and sensate. And *D* brings us to the beloved once again.

There comes a time when the pilgrim on a Celtic path wishes to return. This is the moment when they seek to climb beyond the ordinary and Druid training is begun. At the end of their training, they will take their place to serve the world as a crusader for freedom, unity, and holiness. And they will be in full and sweet partnership with the one created for them from the beginning of time, and with the One, the Godhead. This is the Arthurian promise and the Druid path.

There are three basic phases to this training. These take the disciple through their fears at all levels, in the sensate sheaths, the soul sheaths, and the spirit sheaths. Fear after fear is faced and vanquished in love, until the seeker is a toughened and wise spiritual warrior who can stand calmly and face even the most searing opponents, a leader who can do much to further love's cause on Earth.

There are initiations in this training, and about these we will say little, for this is a path of experience alone. Knowledge and thought only scratch the surface. This is a path that must be lived, its truths embodied. This means that within the range and depth of the seeker's experience, every action and every emotion is used in full awareness and cooperation with love's power. It means these laws are lived so naturally that following them is little different from breathing. The divine laws are fixed, bred, and grown slowly into the very fibers of the individual's being. Then, and only then, will the sweet opening with the One Beloved begin.

The first phase is one in which the seeker glimpses God/Goddess in startling power, and a deep inner connection is formed that will hold and last through all the trials ahead. Then there come fears and steps up the ladder of faith. It is the beginning in which a warriorship of light, filling all darkness, is built, with God/Goddess as support, guide, and friend.

This is the second phase, the courtship phase, where the individual experiences the great love of the One Beloved in sudden opening, in tender and soft moments of pure magic, in crescendos of passion and hopeless longing for full union. It is the sweetest of times and our particular favorite. The spirit world delights in the gradual awakening of the seeker to the experience of being loved, to love's full power, and to the deeply personal nature of the One Beloved's love for him or her. It is a fairy-tale romance between the one and the One Beloved, and all the force of Heaven is brought to bear in bringing through the full and complete awareness of love in this tender and personal way.

During this phase there is initial isolation as the returning pilgrim learns to find intimacy only with spirit, and as the heart stream opens slowly and with joy until it is a rushing torrent between the One and the one. Then, and only then, does the one created for you from the beginning of time come into your life in a real and physical way. Each of you has full memory of the other from eternal realms and full experience of love with the other in physical form, with full awareness that this love comes directly from the Heart of God, the One Beloved, through this physical partner. Each partner is the priest or priestess of the One Beloved's dream for the other, and the intensity and purity of love is beyond mortal comprehension, beyond comprehension of any kind, for it can only be experienced. It is a deep, rich, and satisfying love at the emotional level. A comparable physical experience might be the taste of a slowly melting piece of chocolate of the richest and smoothest order. Full embodiment of love at the highest levels occurs, is fused into the very tissues, is lived, so that the seeker carries this knowledge as naturally as he or she takes a breath.

Then arrives stage three. This is the phase of service. The partners are so bonded in love, their consciousness so joined, that the full force of their love desires some common outlet in service to love's power. They will choose together—for nothing could ever separate them again—a way to give the wellspring of love that has been given them. The visions and missions are varied, both in scope and in direction. But a time will come when sweet communion turns to service. It is a busy and demanding time, but most are so enwrapped in love, they scarcely notice. It is a rewarding time as well and will bring out the full gifts of both partners and apply these with all love's force to the current problems of the Earth. And such is the richness of this part-nered love that the very tides of human endeavor itself will be turned ever so slightly toward love, a turning that cannot be undone.

You have known such partnerships, Franklin Delano and Eleanor Roosevelt's was one. (Many leaders, though, are not at this level; do not suppose all presidents and their wives have attained it.) This gift the partners give is one that, in time, will spread fully across the globe and every single life will be touched and eased by it, for this is the promise of love's reward, the gift of the One Beloved to those who have climbed so hard. The time is fast approaching when multiple partners such as this will be at work across the face of the Earth, and swift will be the changing force of love's power as Earth is lifted and lifted and lifted again.

These are the steps. This threshold, once passed, is a crucial one, where the seeker is then allowed to graduate from the physical Earth, if desired. A choice must be made: to begin again the whole bittersweet journey or to go to one of the higher worlds where fear is unknown and serve from there. First there will be a time of rest and freedom in a place of simple beauty and time to play and take full pleasure in the gentle wonders of this life on Earth. There are many who choose to descend again, to take in a new set of fears and rise through them.

But after the journey has been taken several times, the seeker wishes for a change. It is known to all, this inner fatigue. It becomes clear that the climb ahead will be the final ascent into union, and that at the end of it the seeker will enter Heaven's gate, never to reappear here. There are many who are now at this level in preparation for the great world shift taking place. These understood that the deep inner fatigue would fuel their working through during the necessary tur-moil. To these, the path takes on a special glow. Every element from many, many turns on the wheel of life is brought into play; the full sweetness of love is poured out of the Great Heart to melt the golden pathway the seeker will traverse. This is the fairy tale, the Cinderella-Sleeping Beauty time when deepest fear is replaced by richest love. This is the perfume variety, a specialty of the French Celtic order.

Enough of words. We are deeply honored to serve love's intimate stream with passion, precision, and joy. We wish you all a most heavenly ride in love's chariot and a sure attainment of the happily ever after. We are romantics all and support the full pleasure of love's power.

Our particular helpers in this phase of the ascent, the union phase, are from the plant kingdom. Many are the secret juices, breaths, and essences they create for all of you. You would be amazed if you truly knew the full workings of the natural order. We will speak of them in fifteen families, connected to the fifteen moons of emotional growth, plus Samhain, for understory plants are far more tuned to the lunar cycles than the solar cycles.

We must first describe the separate plant aspects, for, though the plants work as one whole, they are connected to separate nature spirits and have separate overall missions. The three aspects are root, stalk and leaf, and flower or fruit.

The roots in all plants are tended by and co-create with the gnome forces. This family brings the very pregnant inner juices and chemistry of Earth close to the surface for use by the spirit or human world. These inner Earth forces cause rapid and powerful mental openings and have very strong magical powers connected to manifesting one's heart's desires into physical form. Leprechauns, for instance, are of the busy gnomic order tuned to the root chakra of humanity and opening this to the pure flow of the Mother's power.

The juices and chemistry of leaf and stalk belong to the pixie order, members of which are primarily of a masculine nature. Their purpose is one of growth and consciousness, healing, and perfection of form. They can heal all of the body's building blocks: bone, muscle, and connective tissue, as well as the protein and nucleic acid builders. Pixies bring through the male building element. Their forces are particularly attuned to the outer heart, which connects one with others, and are most powerful healers of spinal, chest, arm, and hand disturbances. The stalk and leaf forces could and would work with anyone in bringing full harmony to and between all hearts on Earth. This could be achieved in a very short time for any who is so inclined to dedicate himself to this task.

Flowers are predominately feminine and their force promotes union with the One Beloved. They have a joyful, quiet, sensual nature and their longing for the Sun or the One Beloved to have union with Earth is quite obvious. Flowers are intoxicated with love and longing for union with this One Beloved. They are tended by and work with the flower fairies, also a romantic and sensual order. It is primarily in its essence or perfume where the flower force can be found, and blends of these perfumes can be made to promote such rapid heart openings that all humanity would be amazed. Seeds and fruit are also of this order, but they hold the potential for the future opening of true love, while flower essences bring such opening into the present moment. Flower essences are particularly healing to the deep heart, and the skin, face, hair, and reproductive organs.

These forces are all adapted to the fifteen lunar germination cycles on Earth, plus Samhain—the emotional cycles of growth. There are seasons when varieties of these forces are more potent because of these harmonic influences. Our scribe, because of her many years of gardening and openheartedness to the flower kingdom, has become deeply attuned to the various perfumes and their forces. Her essences are of the highest order, though her belief in herself is not. It is important to note that co-creation between any kingdoms demands a long and loving relationship and cannot be hurried or rushed. Our scribe wishes to say with deep gratitude that it is the flower kingdom, and the flower fairies in particular, who have been so kind and loving to her in her darkest hours that she would not have survived without them—her delicate inner spirit would have closed down completely without their ongoing influence. Here you have an example of an intimate and lifelong relationship with deep trust that brings out the best in both partners.

THE PLANT AND FLOWER FORCES

1. Holly, Wild Rose: December 22–January 15. These are the plants of the first lunar cycle, holly holding the male aspect and wild rose, the female. Holly is the plant of balance and it will help in holding one's center, clarity, and neutrality in any turmoil. Wild rose, especially in this cycle, is the wildness of the inner child, the baby in utero with unlimited potential, and is feminine in nature. Her essence is quite untamed and unbounded and she has a nature that is adverse to direction of any kind. The combination of these is divine, for both qualities are necessary to full attainment of one's divinity.

We do wish to state that it is best when making essences or perfumes to keep the male and females aspects separate until the essence is put to actual use as a tincture. The joining of male and female essence only within the human will bring about the fullest effect.

2. Daisy, Fern: January 16–February 8. The plant families of the second cycle are daisy and fern, particularly asparagus fern. The asparagus fern has quite strong masculine thrusting forces, as is obvious from the shape of the vegetable produced by the plant. It is the plant of rapid growth, the initial thrust of life force, which will eventually blossom during the year to come. Daisy is the feminine plant of friendliness. Its energies are open and willing; it will promote an open mind and an open heart that receives all incoming growth kernels with a warm and welcoming acceptance. This is the time of year when the feminine vessel is germinating the seeds of light for the year's unfoldment.

3. Hellebore, Jack-in-the-pulpit: February 9–March 4. Hellebore or Christmas rose and Jack-in-the-pulpit are both of a watery nature. Jack-in-the-pulpit brings the Mother's watery creator juices into the sacred vessel of the heart. It signifies the uplifting from the unconscious process of germination into the conscious active phase, and it takes the seeds of growth from the female womb to the heart, where they are held in love. This is the second necessary step in creating into manifested reality. The feminine hellebores are able to bloom in the coldest and harshest conditions and their energies will help any and all to believe in a flowering of their own during the darkest nights and most severe struggles of their lives. These two in combination will promote a relationship in which partners do the hard work together, laboring in contentment and patient partnership to bring about birth. It is a sweet and effective essence.

4. Calla lily, Shamrock: March 5–March 28. The families of the fourth cycle are the shamrock and the calla lily, particularly the yellow lily. The shamrock carries the playful leprechaun essence of instant manifestation into physical form. It is male and the plant of absolute magic, in which spirit force takes shape and form in a single moment. Openings into success will come during this time in small, surprising, and playful ways that tempt and tease. But these do not bring about the final openings, which belong instead to the harvest months. The calla is the deep throated feminine who takes the magic of her one beloved and holds it in deep and silent reverence within as she stands in beauty, elegance, and certainty of promises fulfilled. This is a particularly potent combination of essences, for the partnership holds the extremes of serious and holy reverence and playful, teasing magic through which sudden twists and turns can occur amid the deep holding of love's desires.

We would like to state that Easter is another very potent time. The blends of plant forces and the divine are never accidental, but instead are quite precise. You will notice that Easter can fall in the fourth or fifth lunar cycle and that it will have a very different quality depending on where it occurs.

5. Daffodil, Myrtle: March 29–April 21. Families of the fifth cycle are the feminine daffodil and the masculine myrtle. If you notice a daffodil, you may see some slight ridges around the cup. These look similar to candles on a birthday cake or to a family holding hands, and they signal the birth of real action for the year, when the actual form of things to unfold becomes apparent, and when real connections with outer partners in the work begin to be made. This time very much holds a new dawn and springtime, joy-of-new-birth quality. The daffodil is a most happy plant. Myrtle is the plant of patient humility and is also the plant of death. The forces that will break down this unfoldment, then, are set into place at the time of birth. Myrtle holds the force of one who is willing to work tirelessly and in humble service to the divine to accomplish a goal set forth from above, one dear to the seeker's heart. Together these forces bring about groups of co-pilgrims who work well in partnership and can carry the goal through the months of travail ahead into a full harvesting of love's power, a useful union.

6. Tulip, Horsetail: April 22–May 15. The families of the sixth cycle are the feminine tulip and the masculine horsetail. Horsetail carries one of the most ancient essences on Earth. It streams from a time when life here was new and the flow of forces was not so closed. There was a raw intensity to emotion and to living conditions, a wild freedom with many frontiers to be explored, and a new planet of adventures to be experienced. In the spirit world these are known as the green dragon forces and the essence is the wild freedom of love. It is also held strongly in the tails of horses. The tulip, as well, is a passionate essence, although more focused on intimacy and romance. Both of these plant forms bring a passion to the work ahead and passion for the adventure intimacy to be found along the way. Tulip and horsetail taken together are a potent combination and caution is advised.

7. Lily of the Valley, Creeping Jenny: May 16–June 8. The families of the seventh cycle are lily of the valley and creeping Jenny. Despite its feminine name, creeping Jenny is masculine and has a sweet essence of low growth spreading gently but firmly with conscious joy. It is another very happy plant, and the time is one of great joy and love as the first fruits of the early half of the year near completion. There is increasing excitement and a speeding of the pulses as the work comes to a crescendo. Lily of the valley carries a gentle sweetness of the humble feminine. She can be shy and inhabits simple, woodsy places. She is one you can lie beside and one with whom you can let go your inhibitions in trust and simplicity. The sweetness of growing intimacy, as the partners come together in their unfoldment of love's work, is evident in the lily's soft but intoxicating essence. Her holiness becomes pronounced as the union of midsummer draws near.

8. Rose, Mushroom: June 9–July 12. This is the phase when the first half of the annual cycle completes itself at the summer solstice. The families of the eighth cycle are the feminine rose and the mushroom, which holds the masculine power of great expansion from a tiny seed and the musky essence of real and intimate union. The mushroom also carries the true hominess of a male who is in his full divinity here on Earth, humble, warm, and accepting of all. The muskiness comes with the warmth of a full embrace, when penetration of female by male occurs. It signifies an embrace at every level—spirit, soul, and sensate—and completion of this phase of partnership. The rose is the full elegance and beauty of feminine love when that love, again, reaches through spirit and soul into a full physical embrace, when she holds the male within and accepts his seed as a full partner in co-creation within a loving union. The summer solstice is the Earth's outbreath, the time when she is expanded to her full potential. Union at this time takes place at the most expanded levels and the incoming seeds are the impulses of the divine for the remaining six months of the year. But the union is an outer and active one and does not have the solitude and even deeper inner intimacy of the inbreath at the time of the winter solstice. Midsummer's effects are felt primarily in the outer world, as connections with other co-creators in the world.

9. Canterbury Bells, Moss: July 3–July 26. During this ninth lunar phase, there is a turning toward harvest and the slowing down of activity to come, the sense that the hectic days of work will soon wind down to the gathering in of fall and winter's well-earned rest. The families of this cycle are Canterbury bells and moss. Feminine blue-bells, Canterbury bells in particular, are a celebratory strain. They ring out joy for work well done and partnership that has accomplished much of the tasks at hand. Bluebells also carry the first hint of summer's close and the active phase coming to an end. Masculine moss is a holy stream; it lines the walkways to the ancient holy sites and leads all seekers to ancient truths at the end of their inward journey. It signifies the inward walk that commences at this time, as the seeker turns toward the inner sanctum where partnership is with oneself and the One Self of all. Great silence, great holiness, and the return to the internal are its hallmarks. Together these plants lead the celebrant toward home, the male taking the hand of his happy feminine and turning her, ever so slightly, toward the more serious, the deep inner partnership that is theirs alone, bringing the partnership toward the one-on-one phase of true love's call.

10. Sunflower, Yarrow: July 27–August 19. This tenth lunar phase, has as its families the feminine sunflower and all look alikes, such as black-eyed Susans, and Yarrow. The sunflower, is a most joyful plant, for its radiatory love encompasses all the imperfections of the partner, all the dark sides that cannot be hidden through a year's work. It is a plant of embrace and, particularly, acceptance of all darkness and all wounds. It cares not what flaws you may have, it only wants to grin and hold you in love. Yarrow, the masculine plant, flower notwithstanding, has a more serious nature. Its essence is the confidence of a love won, a harvest achieved, and the fullness of love's partnership grown to fruition. There is a dignity in the yarrow's essence—the dignity of love and love's success, as labors of growth turn to gathering in the fruits of that labor and feeling the deep fulfillment of success and security.

11. Monkshood, Aster, Sweet Grass: August 20–September 12. The eleventh lunar phase has for its families the feminine monkshood and aster and the male sweet grass. Monkshood carries the essence of full turning toward the inward self, plus a deep and holy connection to the One through the inner spirit. There is the quieting of self and the power of the mystical to transform at every level. Aster is the flower of the stars. The inner essence is a star in a very real sense, a pentacle when fully developed. Aster holds the memory of being a star child, son or daughter of the One, unique, delicate, and beautiful. Its essence says that you are loved exactly as you are. Sweet grass lays himself at the feet of the female in sweet adoration and honor, as she moves further and further inward to bring some new fullness from her inner co-creator center. These plants together are particularly nourishing to the inner child and bring a readiness to go within and face the inner connection with the One.

12. Gaura, Long Wheat Grass: September 13–October 6. The families of the twelfth cycle are the feminine gaura flower and the masculine long wheat grass. The gentle delicacy of the white gaura flowers suggest the moth, symbol of regeneration and renewal in the light. This phase signifies return to the inner source, striving for inner closeness to the One, the renewal of winter, and the midwinter connection to the One creator force. Wheat grass carries the heavy pregnant fullness of the creator, filled with seeds of light having all the potential of the next cycle of growth. It is a particularly male seed, the fullness of the male ready to impregnate the female again with the seed of the organizing principles of the year to come. This fullness is strong and urgent, a growing sense of his need for release into the female as she approaches the center of her being and the pure channel streaming down from the Source. The grains hold a rich nourishment for the child and the feminine, as well as the male's intense desire to give to both of them. As the delicacy of the female increases, so does the male's urgency to answer her light that shines within, her call for his light, for their two flames to touch again. These two flames once were one and they remember deep in the center of their beings this long-ago ecstasy.

13. Chrysanthemum, Milkweed: October 7–October 30. The families of the thirteenth cycle are the mum and the milkweed plant. The mum is the inner sun of the feminine that has burst its tiny flame and become once again a fiery sun of love for light and for her One True Partner, who is the Source of light and the Source of love. Milkweed is the flight of the male seed out of the cosmic pod of love, or center point, and is the beginning of this seed's journey over the cosmic breath to her. Together these plants bring in a heated pulsing of love's call, a rising need for union in light, union of the One and the one, and a rising need to go indoors and be alone with the Beloved.

14. Blackthorn, Lantern Plant, Low Grass: October 31–November 23. The fourteenth cycle's families are the lantern plant and flowers of the blackthorn, and low grass. The lantern plant, with its orange globes, is the womb of the inner feminine expanded or tented and filled with inner light, which calls to her cosmic love. The blackthorn flower, also feminine, has a deep magnetic quality—like that of Earth Herself—that expresses itself as a longing for light. It is the shadow substance that aches for light, for renewal by love's flame, to receive love's power within. The depth and passion of this inner ache cannot be described, so great is its power. Low grass is a sharp-edged and persistent plant signifying the male who humbles himself to lie low or to stoop to the level of the feminine vessel like a suitor who kneels before his love in abject adoration, to honor her inner beauty, This is the only true approach of male to female.

• Black Rose, Teasel: November 24–November 28. The fifteenth cycle is represented by the black rose and the teasel. This cycle marks the five days of darkness, the intercessory days between the past lunar year and the new one to come, always one month's pulsing before the solar new year at midwinter morning. The black rose signifies the feminine in her darkest phase, when she has a deep and throbbing energy, an intoxication that makes her looser than at other times. Her impulses are a bit stronger, her boundaries are less firm. She dances a seductive and wild tarantella of love as she becomes fully aroused in her desire for union with the One Beloved. Teasel, as its name implies, is a teasing force. It is a bit rough and prickled, and the stimulation of the feminine by this roughness can make her dangerously wild. Great leaps in consciousness are possible at this time, but should be made with caution because fragmentation due to the wildness of the forces must be taken into account. Together these two at this very potent time serve to speed the pulse of the female and deepen her desire for receiving.

15. Rosemary, Laurel, Bay: November 29–December 20. The sixteenth and final lunar cycle is represented by the feminine rosemary and laurel, and the masculine bay. Rosemary is the quintessential plant of the feminine who has danced with her beloved and now lays herself down in quiet and gentle receptivity, all her wildness spent. A calm and sweet pattern of holding comes over her. She is an exceptionally sweet and mild plant. Laurel, of course, brings the peace of the feminine who has danced and played and now waits in quietness for him to enter her. She is obedient and receptive, a feminine in full surrender and holiness to the divine. Bay brings a muskiness and strong masculine odor to the mix. It signifies the increasing power and confidence of the male as his impulse speeds ever nearer His beloved Earth and She who waits to receive Him.

• **Mistletoe, December 21.** The union of light from the Highest Source and from Earth occurs on midwinter morning, as the rays of the sun come in, now fully aligned with the open portals to higher ray levels. This missile of light anchors fully in the feet or toes! The incoming seeds of light, the organizing nucleic principles, are anchored deep within all feminine vessels on Earth, within the womb, to gestate and germinate for later growth into form. The plant for this union is the mistletoe, so beloved by all Druids as the plant holding resonance with this highest Source of light.

It is with joy in our partnership here on our beloved Earth that the plant and flower kingdoms work to further the great plan of the divine. We are honored to serve and we delight in our gentle, but powerful infusions that help to heal, instruct, and transform all mankind. We, too, look forward with delight to increasing consciousness of the co-creation possible between ourselves and all humanity. Our blessings are ever around you as you unfold on your way.

We, the flower kingdom, ask you, while you keep us in your homes or at work, to note the placement of the crown energies at the tops of our stems, just beneath the flower and supporting it. The stem and stalk are always a male energy, the flower always female. We would like you to notice how the male in the plant kingdom works to support the feminine in her full flowering into union with the One. It is this attitude that could greatly speed the opening on Earth—the male in service of and support to the feminine—for she is the inner bridge to union and is the embodiment of the divine. We hope our example of the great beauty of the flowering feminine in her co-creation with the light will serve as a helpful example to all mankind. The masculine, rather than the feminine, is in service to the inner spirit or essence of light. All sensate functions must and will be subdued and disciplined to serve these inner union pulses, and great will be the leaps and growth in consciousness when this occurs. Union happens on the inside between creator and created, and it is the most powerful force in the cosmos. True union is not, as so many feel, with the outer beloved in form. Let this speak to all who care to listen. Good journey and good day.

8

Father Sun, Mother Moon: Transformation

The Celtic lunar cycle is the cycle of emotional growth and is on the twenty-four-day lunar cycle and the fifteen-month form, plus five intercessory days. In actuality, it is a Mother-Child cycle, committed to helping humanity, all the Mother's children, transform the unconscious shadow self into the wisdom or blue ray child. All blue ray or indigo children now coming into the planet have obtained their wisdom levels in previous lifetimes. The Mother's rhythms follow the growth pattern of plants and the inner gestational cycle of the human birth process. The moon is the queen or ruler of these forces and oversees all growth through clearing, via experience, the unconscious illusions or fear-based beliefs on the Earth plane. Her mission is to see that all Earth's children achieve their wisdom status, at which point the Father's growth cycle becomes more predominant through the Logos planes, until the Arthurian center point is reached.

When the Arthurian level is completed, the divine feminine and divine masculine co-create, according to a blending of the Gregorian-Celtic calendar, to manifest their deepest heart's desires in pure love and service, in accordance with the overall planetary growth moved forward by the Logos. The Julian-Gregorian Father's cycle is an animal husbandry cycle. The Celtic Mother is a plant and germination cycle, and it would ease much if animal care and agriculture were brought into alignment with these cyclic time tables.

The Mother's way is the way of experience. She teaches through life lessons in an experiential and hands-on manner. The resulting change in consciousness is gradual, natural, and unconscious, as is the plant growth pattern. She is firmly in charge of the unconscious and leads each individual through the wisdom lessons they have chosen for each lifetime. Her rules are firm and Her force powerful. Struggle is entirely useless and only increases the pain, for the entire life force moves in the direction of this self-chosen growth.

The Mother's yearly cycle begins after the five intercessory days, which end on November 28; the first quadrant is committed to the inner essence. There is a gathering of the Mother's creative juices from the broken down forms of the old year. Then comes the impregnation of the nuclear organizing light symbols on the morning of the midwinter solstice. These symbols are nuclear in nature and of a Christ essence. From within the Mother's Womb they influence all nuclear patterning for the following year, the patterns of evolution that will unfold in the manifested experiences of the year to come. The Mother is in full receptivity and surrender to the Father's plan and Kingdom and holds these light seeds within Her creative juices in a deep and peaceful love. This is the physical union in the great co-creative sexual cycle of Sun and Earth.

During the next twenty-four–day lunar period, the **Birch Moon,** December 22 through January 15, the first beginnings of unfoldment will be seen. A single overall purpose or mission is fused into place within the growing physical form of all beings and will serve as the central axis and direction of force for the year's growth. This first quadrant involves growth of the inner little girl or the inner spirit essence, which is impressed by the new force for growth.

In the next lunar cycle, the **Rowan Moon,** January 16 through February 8, the Father's influence will come into play. Firm laws and boundaries of growth will be put into place, and the conscious or intellectual pattern will begin to unfold from the nuclear seed in the womb. This will reveal the actual structure coming into flesh out of the single principle of growth.

During this cycle comes the high Celtic festival of Brigid, Imbolc, on February 5, when the Mother, who is the shepherdess leading the young lamb, takes over. Growth becomes predominately that of the little boy aspect. He covers the inner essence with a specific identify, the nature of the person bringing the impulse of growth into the outer world, so the two work as one. This is a birth impulse.

The **Ash Moon** of February 9 through March 4 brings the opening and expansion of growth from the confines of the womb and the structures of the Father. A childlike, playful aspect appears, and a building of activity toward outer work/play and accomplishment is revealed. This is the stretching impulse of the child.

The **Alder Moon,** March 5 through March 28, carries the spurting exuberance of the boy and a great increase in energy, enthusiasm, and activity for the yearly goals. The vernal equinox is the morning when the boy brings into the mix the Mother's juices, carried up from the Earth. In plants this comes in the form of sap, the Mother's juices brought into specific form by the boy.

The **Black Willow Moon,** March 29 through April 21, is the Great Mother impulse. Her creator juices are drawn up from the Earth and there is a great flowering of form into varied outer expressions. Her rich passion and pleasure are added to the unfoldment process.

The **Hawthorne Moon,** April 22 through May 15, is a time of purity and perfection as the forms are manifested, new and fresh, in outer reality. The second high Celtic festival occurs at this time on May 5—Beltane. It is the festival of the bride or virgin, still perfect and untouched, the eternal beauty of the feminine form. This marks the shift of the growth into the masculine quadrant, or action in the outer world.

The period of May 16 through June 8 ushers in the **Oak Moon,** moon of the beloved. This is the time when the male force joins the female, the union of male and virgin. It brings a true manifestation of the form for the year's growth, the first fruits of the gestation process and the sweetness of satisfaction.

June 9 through July 2 is the time of the **Holly Moon,** cycle of the warrior, the chivalric male who pushes for justice, truth, and protection of women and children. Great strides in the year's work are often made during this time, when the strength of the male force is at its greatest. On the summer solstice is revealed the Beloved King aspect of the male, the actual structure of full growth mixed with the pushing energy of the warrior. This is a powerful and productive time.

The **Hazel Moon** follows, July 3 through 26, when female spiritual powers are added to the mix: Prophecy, intuition, and a close connection to the spirit world are strong influences during this time. A clear vision of the remaining cycle and the barest beginning of the following year are put into place. Revealed are the boundaries of what can be accomplished in the remaining months and a redefinition of the specific form the year's completion will take.

July 27 through August 19 brings the **Apple Moon** of the mature feminine. It brings into manifestation the first fruits of the year's labor and initiative. This is the time of satisfaction and fruition. On August 5 comes the third high Celtic festival, Lughnasa, signaling completion of the masculine quarter and the shift into the Mother's quadrant, which will bring the full manifestation of the year's growth.

The **Vine Moon,** August 20 through September 12, is a time of sweetness and intoxication, when the intense laboring begins to slow and the time for family and partnership is increased. It brings sweet communion of male and female when labors are done.

September 13 through October 6 is the time of the **Ivy Moon,** Goddess time, when the Mother draws back all into reunion, beginning with each family and partners at their own hearths. There is a coming together in leisure and celebration. The autumnal equinox is the time when male and female come together after their active labors, and there is rest and closeness once more.

The period of October 7 through October 30 is that of the **Reed** or **Cattail Moon.** It is a time for community and celebration of the whole together, drawn back to the bosom of the Mother into closeness and community.

And, finally, comes the **Blackthorn Moon,** October 31–November 23. This is the great time of completion. Remaining debts are paid, loose ends tied up, all that has not been done is finished and the year's pattern closed off and ended. New mysteries ready for unfoldment are gathered in readiness for the new cycle about to begin.

The five intercessory days or festival of Samhain, November 24–28, are the time of great recycling. The nuclear patterns of manifestation are recalled into the Great Womb, and all structures are broken down and renewed for the beginning and building of another cycle.

Next comes the **Elder Moon,** November 29 through December 21, when the wisdom growth for the completed year becomes fused into the soul and spirit structures and all remaining confusions of the past year are cleared away. The new dominant pattern is then put into place. These fused lessons stay with the evolving form into eternity and become part of the cosmic wisdom reservoir. They also determine the plane this form will return to after death.

The Mother's rhythms are dominant in all emotional growth and in the feminine gestation and reproductive hormonal cycles. Regulating the feminine system to the twenty-four–day pattern, rather than to the distorted twenty-eight–day cycle, would go far in relieving stresses currently placed on the feminine form in each human and on the planet as a whole.

The Mother's influence is primarily felt in the lower four chakras as unconscious shadow or fear beliefs of the child and young adult are brought to the attention of the seeker for purification and healing, and as truths becoming manifest in the heart. The planet's chakras are structured precisely the same way as human chakras, so that the deep and early wounds of humanity are played out in the southern hemisphere and learning occurs there more predominantly through emotional experience. This can be seen in the emphasis in the southern hemispheres on family, community, play, and magic.

Time of birth and its alignment with the Celtic calendar will tell each individual what aspect of self they are strengthening or perfecting in that life, and which impulse of the Mother they will be particularly influenced by in their own emotional growth. The Mother, or the feminine, rules the left side of the heart and will set the tone for the emotional experience of that life in partnerships and nuclear families. This completes the Mother's cycle.

The Father's influence is in the top four chakras and oversees conscious linear growth through knowledge, personal identity, and work in the outer world. His influence predominates in the northern hemisphere, with its cultural emphasis on work and action. He rules the right side of the heart.

The Mother's influence can be seen in all indigenous religions, with their worship of nature, song, dance, intuition, magic, direct communication with the spirit world, community, and sexuality. The Father's influence is seen in organized religions, with their emphasis on law, direct paths to truth, and established structures of both church and tradition. The day approaches when all will come together and work as one whole and holy body, with both sides honoring, learning from, and co-creating with each other.

The guardians and workers within the Mother's cycle are crystals. Each of the fifteen lunar months, plus Samhain, has a crystal family committed to that cycle's mission and these will be reviewed briefly. Each crystal is connected to a star system, also dedicated to bringing forth this aspect of the mystery.

CRYSTAL FAMILIES ASSOCIATED
WITH THE LUNAR MONTHS

1. Clear Quartz, December 21–January 15. The crystal of Midwinter and the Birch Moon is clear quartz, a structure that focuses the gentle Christ essence and heals all deep wounds, especially those of the inner child. This crystal channels a potent and focused beam of the Christ power, which will penetrate into virtually any darkness and gently and gradually dissipate the fear force being held there. It connects to the star system Sirius.

2. Feldspar, January 16–February 8. The crystal of the Rowan Moon is feldspar, rich in the silicate base of the Father's Kingdom. These crystals hold memories of paradise and the child freed from its slavery to fear. The feldspars connect to the star field of Orion.

3. Calcite, February 9–March 4. The Ash Moon's companion crystal is calcite. This mineral is rich in the memory of freedom and growth without the impediment of fear, nestled within a framework of absolute security of love of parents for the child. It is a powerfully healing stone and connects to the star system Sirius.

4. Obsidian, March 5–March 28. The Alder Moon's companion stone is obsidian, both the black and particularly the underlying clear turquoise blue. These connect to the deep cosmic force of the Mother's ocean and to Her essence brought forth in the boy's spouting exuberance for action. This essence is held in all sea creatures as well, especially in dolphins and whales. It connects to the star system Orion.

5. Slate, March 29–April 21. The Black Willow Moon's mineral resonance is with slate, a combination of the Mother's fresh watery flow and the slow wisdom climb, layered like stony sediment steps through eons of suffering and growth. All the muck of fear is held in love and gentleness here, waiting for growth and restructuring to a higher level to occur. This stone connects to Earth.

6. Diamond, April 22–May 15. The Hawthorn Moon's crystalline companion is diamond, a stone that shows the clarity and purity of the feminine as she truly is. Held within it is her holiness, her powers to cleanse and to reflect the Father's truth in brilliance, and a withstanding force of love that can survive all disruption and any pain with renewal and radiance. It is a most magical stone and connects to the star system Cassiopeia.

7. Granite, May 16–June 8. The stone of the Oak Moon is granite, a fusion of the structure of law and the slow heated growth of struggles and pressures over long periods of time, forged into a world warrior of truth and justice. It brings forth the male beloved of all, champion of the child and the feminine, and connects to the star system Orion.

8. Cairngorm, June 9–July 2. The stone of the Holly Moon is cairngorm, especially the blood-red variety. This stone carries the imprint of the sacrifice of the male who is forced to become a child soldier, to fight brother, and to be killed. It bears the mark of the extreme sacrifice for love: one's life given in its totality. It is a most honorable stone and connects to the star system Orion.

9. Moonstone, July 3–July 26. The Hazel Moon's mineral companion is moonstone, the milky essence holding a true and clear connection to the spirit realms and to future mysteries waiting to be revealed. It will reveal only that which is allowed. Much is kept unseen, for the Father is quite a lover of sweet surprise. It connects both to the Moon and the star system Cassiopeia.

10. Rutile, July 27–August 19. The Apple Moon's companion stone is rutile, a mineral full of the complete flowering of the feminine powers. In this feminine she is wise in her maturity, standing in her own truth, fully in her power of intuition, able to manifest her desires into reality, and rich in her passion and honoring of the masculine as well as the feminine. It connects to the star system Andromeda.

11. Ruby, August 20–September 12. The Vine Moon's companion stone is Ruby, signifying the intoxication of the fulfilled. The goals have been achieved, the harvest gathered in, and the time of togetherness and pleasure and the victory of work well done is at hand. It connects to the star system Arcturus.

12. Chrysoprase, September 13–October 6. The stone of the Ivy Moon is chrysoprase, a deep-seeded crystal stream rising to the surface under the stress and tensions of adversity. It carries the imprint of the patient endurance of the Mother birthing her child of light through the long cycles of pain. It will help all in need of endurance during suffering. It connects to the star system Orion.

13. Marble, October 7–October 30. The stone of the Reed Moon is marble, a blending of many colors, many streams into the fullness of community achieved. It takes a deep knowing of others with patient growth in holiness and peace to achieve such group beauty and the overflowing of joy and celebration that comes forth. It is a most holy stone connecting to the star system Arcturus and the constellation of the Great Bear.

14. Opal, October 31–November 23. The stone of the Blackthorn Moon is Opal. It holds the power to manifest deep desires into form as well as the attendant responsibility of the user for all magic, whether black, with its rebound and ferocity, or white, which surrounds in gentle joy. Beware the temptation to create on your own outside the higher mind, for this will harm you. This stone connects to the star system Arcturus.

• Plutonium, November 24–November 28 (Samhain). The stone of the five intercessory days is the philosopher's stone, plutonium, stone of the plutonian forces for transmutation, with their grids holding one plane of form separate from another. It can take any to the next higher level but will cause great gifting or harm, according to the will and intention of the user. Be doubly careful with this stone. It connects to the cosmic black hole, entrance to the Mother's Womb.

15. Uranium, November 29–December 20. The crystal of the Elder Moon is uranium, a potent creator crystal that can mutate genetic material, one of very few forms as powerful as The Father's nuclear genetic force. The uranium family is most eager for humankind to become conscious and responsible for the use of this powerful mineral and wishes to say that they are eager to transform the current misuse of their powers for destructive purposes. Uranium connects to the star system Orion.

We have only a brief caution in wisdom that remains. The mineral kingdom is in alignment with the astrological cycles and the forces of transmutation supporting a return to the Source and the great moving force of time. We hold the deepest and most transformative powers, for we can take you through all grids holding the planes of form and their structures in place, separated from each other. We are in loving service to humanity and can be used in powerful ways to heal, shift, transmute, and enlighten. We have carried you all down from the heights through your descent to the deepest levels, and we know the way back again. For those wishing a direct path to enlightenment, see the stones.

We of the mineral kingdom are the transmutation of plutonian forces and we regulate all cycles within the time-space continuum. Many there are who would use our powers to gain a forced upper hand for money or personal power. This variance has been allowed since the crystalline betrayal of love, late in Atlantean times. Once we came through the barrier at the dawn of this millennium, signaling the end of the dominance of darkness, all such variance will no longer be allowed. Any who attempt to force the mineral or astrological kingdoms to betray their service to love and serve personal power once more will experience a swift and severe rebound against themselves. We refer to all military purposes for these elements, the use of outer space, and the use of any black magic with crystalline forces who are in full service to love and love alone. The rebound is a teaching and a warning, not a punishment.

All who are working with a conscious loving intent to move

through the shift and with the greater good in their hearts will be protected and lead by the spirit world. Those who hold onto destructive and negative fear-based structures will not survive. We are sorry for this, but it is time for Heaven to arrive and all must chose who they will serve: fear or love.

The force of love will prevail and it wishes to birth creator partnerships based in the God/Goddess experience of co-creating one's heart's desires into reality through sacred sexual union. This is the Arthurian fulfillment. These partnerships must be based fully in love within holistic communities dedicated to: sustainability, simplicity, self-empowerment, and technology to benefit the All in line with the greater good. We cannot and would not stop these changes, for it is time for darkness finally to be overthrown. Make all choices wisely, for there could be many who do not succeed in this return to love. As the leaders lead, so it will be done to the people they rule, and visa versa. It is time to take responsibility for yourselves, to stand up and speak out for love and love alone. It is not an easy climb. We hold all humanity in great honor and wish you well. It is our joy to serve on this return to love. Be blessed.

One more word. There is a creator substance that remains undiscovered. Once found, it can and will rapidly change your world. Only those fully anchored in love's power will know the great fulfillment of truth that will come through this stone. It will be discovered in the United States. We love you all.

9

The Mother's Kingdom:
Peace on Earth, Creativity, and Love

The Mother's Kingdom is a place where we have all lived before, from which all humanity has descended. The laws at the beginning of this book are sacred and holy there. There one can see and speak with spirit forms and all things; communicate telepathically, which is as easy as— or more easy than—speaking; and work out any and all arrangements with fairness and mercy. It was an idyllic place before the fracturing began. The hallmark of this land was united couples, male and female, who ruled their own households and families with absolute integrity, equality, and justice. It was a delightful place where all things were alive, the peaceable kingdom. Fear was unknown. This was the Otherworld of some renown in the Celtic consciousness, the way of descent for all whose motherland is in Europe and the British Isles. Other cultures have their own traditions, stories of the descent, but these do not concern us here. It was during the fragmenting warfare of Celtic times that this world gradually disappeared.

We, keepers of this realm, stand nearby, on the other side of the veil that separates our world from yours. Your dear, departed loved ones also live here and call it Heaven. We wish to speak with you who remain trapped in the world of fear, primarily because we want to offer to work with you. Because this is a place of absolute joy and security, where fear is unknown, we can send you transmissions, either telepathically or energetically, that can help you tremendously on your climb to freedom, your return to light. In fact, this climb is so difficult and sometimes perilous that few can make it without our help. This Otherworld was created and is ordered and ruled over by Divine Mother and Divine Father, and these two are presided over by the gentle Christ. All three—and all of you—are forms taken by and are expressing the One Beloved God.

We come now to ask each of you to chose two guides, one male and one female, to help you in your travail of birthing your Divine Child. This child is a long ago part of you that you know and actually can live out more comfortably than any other aspect within you. But many fears, even terrors, stand in your way to being who you truly are. Because we can clearly see your spirit form and all the fears in their ordered patterns surrounding it, we can guide you, with gentleness and strength, through each one in its proper turn. These are things you cannot do for yourself so easily. We are many here: tree, plant, animal, water, fire, stone, angel, devic gods and goddesses (all lesser than the One Beloved God, of course, of whose body we are all a part). We are asking each one of you to find some way to connect with us through the hearts and consciousness of one male and one female guide. These guides do not need to be permanent; you may wish to change them in your climb and this is fine, even perfect. Just let us know.

We are here to serve you. We remember quite consciously the time when we could see and speak together, when all were one. And because the great rift of fear came between us, we can only see but not speak to you, and you do not see us at all. This puts us in great sorrow, for you are our brothers and sisters and we remember each of you as family. Imagine what it would be like if you found yourself invisible to all your own family! How sad and disturbing it would be to try to talk, to reach out and hug, and yet get no reaction at all. Great is our love for you.

Many of you think of us and try to remember or read books or meditate very hard. Some, such as our scribe and friend, can finally, after years of clearing work, see us dimly, hear our voices, feel our hearts. It is a great blessing.

But we want you back, too. We want to be visible to everyone. We want you all. For those who chose to descend into the worlds of fear, it is time now to come Home to where you truly belong, with heart and mind opened to the consciousness of love. We wait with trembling hearts and brimming eyes for the day when this will be, when the veil gradually disappears, and we can once more be one family and can see and touch you. Achieving this is our overriding purpose and heart's desire. We work for this night and day, sending energies of love, whispering blessings and memories from our world to yours, implanting memories of love and hope and tenderness in the grasses where you may walk, the books you may read, the food you eat. It is all we can do. Interference is never allowed.

But now, because of all the clearing work and the ascension so many are working toward, the veil is actually thinning. There are some who can reach us and actually feel held in love. We hold them with tears of joy streaming down our cheeks. We long to hold you, too— everyone. Some of us who remember you are your true and loving families from the star you were created on. Our longing to love you is great. Because the veil has thinned, we are asking all of you, even those who haven't contacted the spirit world before, not since you were a young child, perhaps: Please choose a form where we can come to you—a special tree, a dog, a stone. Or choose a favorite angel who can come, but then we're back to not being able to be seen by you and not being able to touch you. Because nature did not descend into fear, all of us can fuse temporarily with a tree, for instance. We are made of light so it's quite easy, and the trees or stones or flowers are so happy to oblige. They long to bring you Home, too. We all do.

Pick a special nature friend and ask your guides to come and meet you there half an hour a day, maybe more. Because the world is moving into great changes and everyone must face many fears to build their child of light, there could come scary times. We want everyone, we don't want a single person to be left out, but the climb is hard and the fears can be intense. You will need our help. So, please, today or tomorrow, without delay, choose two guides and a form in which they can meet you, any one you like, any form. It could be Christ and Mother Mary who come to you, in a bush or favorite flower. It could be your own guardian angels, whomever you trust—just come and talk with us. Don't worry if everyone chooses the same guides. In spirit form we can be with all at once. This may be hard for you to understand, but one day you will see.

We have a plan to bring you Home, to melt the great veil that separates your realm of fear from ours of love. For the veil to disappear, everyone must help, for each person's consciousness contributes to it. Even if two thirds of the world faced all their fears, one third of the veil would remain because the veil belongs to all. We've been thinking and praying and conferring. Here's our plan:

We ask you to come and make friends with your chosen guides, whoever you want them to be. Make a commitment to this relationship even when you can't see them. We promise you that quite quickly you will feel in your heart what they are sending you, that you are surrounded by a loving presence. We promise you. But you must come-for a half hour each day. It is all right to pick a form outside in nature for summer and a form inside your home or office for winter. It's perfectly all right. Just let us know. We want you to be comfortable.

When you come to the spirit, speak to us of your hopes and your dreams, the deep desires you feel in your heart. We will begin to create these for you, the path of fears you need to clear to achieve your chosen hopes. We promise you. When you feel trusting enough, speak to us of your pain, your disappointments, the dark hurts of your life. Just gather up the disappointments of each day and give them to us.

We know how to make them go away, we know how to put them into the bright light that transforms them and turns them into love.

Then we will teach you how to do this for yourself. You each have a perfect spark deep in your child heart. It is pure and holy and can hold anything at all—murder, rape, incest, torture, madness, loneliness, poverty, and insanity, the worst things you have endured—and can transform it into love and truth. We so much wish to help you, each and everyone. We love you so! Bring your fears, a few each day, and you will feel very soon how quickly they begin to transform.

We can tell when you have brought most of your current trials and then we will take you to the next level, through all the fears you lived through as you've descended through soul levels. There are many here and the fears can be intense. It is perhaps the hardest stage of ascension. For a man, these will be pushing and driving forces, failure at work; for a woman, they might be aggression and sexual oppression and carrying too much responsibility. For both, there will be fears of betrayal of love and financial strain. Just keep giving them to us or let us show you how to melt the fears in your heart of hearts and all will be well. It will take some time, a year or two, and there will be pain. But you will come to see that you are not responsible for anyone else, only yourself, and how this clearing work frees you from the heavy load of having to take care of everyone else and be what they need. It will take you well on your way to transformation.

When this level is done, you will shift to spirit levels. It is a magical time, for it is at this point that you will begin to see us in your inner mind. We can come to you quite clearly in your thoughts. Many reconnections to spirit worlds will open to you. Some very special and magical work will be given to you to do. You will begin to learn and to prepare for a great gift to the world. But this will also be a time when you are quite alone. There is hard work and isolation in continuing your daily clearing work. There are many disrupting forces and you will learn that creating the timing and the details is not up to you but comes from the Mother and the Father, who are taking care of you. The driving, overwork forces will clear. Again, it takes time. New friends and connections will emerge and your great work will begin. It is a holy and exciting time.

Then comes the connection to the One Beloved, who is God. This is the time of sweetness. There will be days that you will spend weeping with joy, when the great Source of Love surrounds you. And there will again be days of fear and pain. There is continued financial strain, though less than before, and there are failure and defeat. Strong fragmenting forces of the mind come in—depression, paranoia—and these you will learn to melt in love, slowly and surely, one after another, until you are free and there is peace.

Slowly the deep heart panic of never finding love at all, of no security, of not knowing how to manifest your dreams, will disappear. Slowly your work will grow. You will learn to let go of all the many details of the past and future and just be, to let the day and moment you are living in be enough. That is when the world truly comes alive, when focus brings such rich vividness around you. You'll feel like a child again, led by the gentle Christ and all His forces of love, and you will know connection with the other side. And then the magic will begin, for you will see all things, inner and outer, as the One Body of your Beloved God and finally begin to love all things and know all as the One. Respect and courtesy will come naturally. You will see yourself as a spark of Christ and feel an inkling of your truth, your great beauty and capacity for love.

And then the one created for you, actually that one who was created in the same moment as you, will appear. There will still be trials, trials of romance, of holding back, of the slow opening of this miracle. Many have climbed through so much difficulty at this point. They fall into impatience and sometimes despair. But never fear, for this is the stage when true love comes. Already you know the spiritual supports that always come: You have felt their empowerment of the true you; the gift of a great work to do; and old, old spirit friends who have begun to appear and nourish you. So, there is a strong faith and feeling of God. But this one person is your own true love, created just for you, the sweetest gift of all. It will take time, and yes, there are more obstacles to overcome, but love will open and flower.

You will be to each other the pure true love of God, so clear that it comes from the very Source of love through you. You will live in holy partnership, and through your sacred sexual union, you will create into manifested reality your own heart's desires. For both of you together it is a most magical time. It is the God/Goddess experience, for this is precisely how your Mother and Father created all of you and all of us, and all worlds, everything that happens. You will know the great ecstasy of love fulfilled, the passion and everlasting security, the peace of holy familyhood. You will feel and be divine, created in your Parents' image.

This is perhaps your Beloved's finest gift to you and was the entire purpose of your descent. All fear was made simply to create a separate identity for yourself, a separate consciousness. It is an experience we, who did not descend, can never know, for you will feel in your own beloved the consciousness of the Beloved Christ in flesh. The physical is something we in spirit form cannot know. You will come to understand that all those fears simply slowed down your spirit enough to freeze its light into flesh, so that you could be in a body and touch through skin and flesh. What a miracle your physical form is, your skin, your sensation of touch and taste and movement. When you have cleared enough so that all you see and feel is love, this gift will become the amazing miracle that it was meant to be. Can you imagine feeling your Beloved God in every bite you eat, in every sight you see, in every person, particularly in your own true love? This will come to be. Humanity will weep with joy and kneel in gratitude for long and long. And this is where we lead you! All will recognize the outer and the inner simply as different forms of the One Beloved Christ, the One Body made manifest in a rich variety, and love will rise across the lands and flood the Earth with so much joy! You will be amazed! This is where we lead you. So, do not despair in your fear and your pain on your climb. All will be well.

At the end of the climb you will give your great gift. Again, obstacles will come and must be faced. It will not be an easy time. But you will face them together with your own true love and be held in your distress. You see how your God lets you experience the fullness of Himself/Herself?

And then you will be free. Communities will form very naturally. All you need will simply come together—not glamorous housing, no, but the magnificence of nature and simple homes will surround you. Simple homes, simple pleasures, singing, praying, dancing—you will have it all, great intimacy, great inner strength and identity, great achievements, and a peaceful community of simple folk in simple love of All.

Then, and only then, will the veil lift and disappear. Hurrah! How great will our own joy be then! To see you and hug you and speak, after all these ages of time watching you in all your trials and pain. Hurrah, we say! This is God's plan for you, all the children of the One Beloved Christ who created you and who loves you each so tenderly. His and Magdalene's, His Bride's, dearest wish is for you to be fulfilled. Both long to lead you Home to joy abounding. All will be well.

§ 10 §

Community and Family:
Freedom of the Spirit Child

Each person, when their travail is complete, will come to live in a community created by the Father and Mother just for them. It will feel like the village in Heaven you were created into eons ago. Your heart remembers this place and the pure joy you knew there. Many details will be created to open this memory for each of you.

You will have a small and simple dwelling place, easy to care for, easy to build, easy to repair, so it will nurture but never bind you. The design will be the same as the little home you first knew in Heaven. To those who are drawn to this book, you were created into the Celtic realms. These are real places in Heaven and are most like the farming and fishing villages of the Hebrides or the western Irish shore. The deep memory of security, being richly nourished by Mother, Father, and Christ will be restored. You will want for nothing and all will be done as a community: house building, food growing, even cooking, and for the Celtic descendants especially, there will be poetry, dance, and song. You will know simple ways; a deep reverence and consciousness of the Christ in all things; and with all others, a peace and mutual courtesy that is now unknown. You will live in small cottages by the sea and have hands-on connection to the life of this community, surrounded by family who descended with you and whom you have known over and over in many forms, as brother and sister, as mother and father, as son and daughter, and lover, too. The loving nourishment from every lifetime all the way back to eternity will surround you.

At first, the most severely wounded of the world, those who once belonged to you will come, and the healers among you will heal them or teach them to heal themselves. But after this short phase, war and illness will be unknown, a gentle loving peace will be restored, and harmony and joy will reign on Earth once more. A time of rest and restoration will come upon you and the memory of Heaven will once more be reality. This peace has the power to heal all divisions among you and to remove even the memory of pain. Religions will honor each other, the purpose of the various sacred streams will be known and revered. Muslim will pray for Jew, Christian for Native American or African—all are the same. A long time of peace will anchor in the Earth plane and all things will be healed. To those who have suffered so on their journey to individual creatorhood, a long sweet drink of love will be given: a thousand years. This has been decreed by the Father and Mother. Nothing can stand in its way.

There are certain laws of community that must be embodied and followed before these villages can materialize and these we would like to share with you. The understandings will help you in your trials of growth.

Laws of Community

1. All things are the Body of God, the One Beloved Christ/Magdalene. All contain His/Her mysterious purposes waiting to be revealed and His/Her magnificent radiance. All are to be honored and revered.

2. All beings are independent and sovereign over their own fields of sway. Even stinkbugs have a sacred purpose and

all must be honored and worked with in courtesy and respect.

3. Any and all agreements must be good for everyone involved. Winning and losing will not be supported. A mutuality of gifting will always be necessary. If, for instance, you are requesting that an ant move out of your house or a deer leave your crops undisturbed, you must give them something in return, with honor and gratitude.

4. The One Beloved is the head of All. Any and all tensions, disagreements, or disturbances of any kind will be solved in consultation with His/Her consciousness, and His/Her suggestions will hold precedence.

5. Group consciousness reveals itself equally through all participants. To understand movement toward change or growth, the suggestions of all must be heard and held in the mind and heart of each, and then a group consensus reached. This point is particularly important, for it contains the heart threads of everyone. If any one is left out, that one heart begins to retreat. It is the hearts that hold the whole together. Any retreat will begin a fragmentation process that grows harder and harder to reverse, as you who fell know well.

6. No interference with the process or choice of any other is ever allowed. Again, this is one of the cardinal rules and the breaking of it is the force most responsible for evil in your world as it is now. This is particularly true in the realm of spiritual belief, connection, and worship. All choices of how, when, and who to worship will be made by each individual alone or with Christ/Magdalene. This individual spirit connection is to be the most revered, for it keeps the individual beloved connection open to the One Beloved Christ. It is this holiest of places that keeps all

alive. This will come to be understood. The great power of silence and being will become known. If the One Beloved comes with a message of pain, it simply means an inner healing is necessary and is not a signal to change in any way the one who brings the message. That other is responsible for himself or herself.

7. The community, with all work and positions of leadership, will function like a living organism. All will be chosen for certain jobs through prayer and in deference to the will of the One Beloved. The length of time an individual serves will also be given by the One Beloved, and all will in truth serve Him/Her. Leadership is not taking charge but is rather serving the whole. Mark this well.

8. Any who persist in anger, negativity, blame, divisiveness, or gossip will be given a chance to choose love and to heal. Should they persist in their negative ways, they must be asked to leave. Sadly, this is sometimes necessary to keep the One Body healthy.

9. Creator powers must be aligned to the greater good. All sexual partnerships will be understood as co-creative, with the flow of love coming from the very highest Beloved levels of the Godhead. These will be held in the utmost of respect, within an equal balance of self and other love giving and receiving. These will be understood as the highest and most holy ways one can be connected and in service to another. Every interaction will be brought through with holiness and reverence for the great love. The lack of discipline and mastery over these intense sexual co-creator streams will be brought into alignment with and subdued by the sweet Christ power and will. All aspects of sexual partnerships will be fully in tune with the will of the divine. This includes partner choice, timing, the

absence of force of any kind, mutual respect, reverence for the other, and service to love of the highest order. Such sacred sexual unions will be understood as one of the most sacred expressions of love and will never be interfered with in any way.

10.   There will be cooperation with, relaxation into, and understanding of the natural order and flow. Simplicity, sustainability, and mutually cooperative respect with the natural world will come about. Planting, building, celebration, and growth will follow the astrological, solar, and lunar cycles. All these will be felt and understood, as will all messages from nature. Such cooperation and understanding will bring a slow and unhurried pace to all life and all endeavor.

11.   Each person will be given one great gift with which to return his love to Earth and his global family in gratitude for all blessings of each life. This special talent will be obvious from childhood and will be honored and supported by family, school, and community at large. Education will be revolutionized and simplified into a hands-on experience of the natural order and cycles. It will bring full integration into the life and pulse of the One Body of this community, an expression of one's talents into full unfoldment, and the offering of teachers who can attend each student's growth to mastery. Teaching, like leadership, is again not taking charge, but rather is a service to the student. Often it will be the student who will lead.

12.   Celebration, worship, community bonding, and praise to Mother, Father, and Christ/Magdalene will be regular and simple but highly developed. They will include: community-wide meals, song, dance, worship, prayer, storytelling, poetry, art fairs, healing, and more. These times are more

important than you currently know and are necessary to bring and keep the One Body within a cohesive wholeness. Lack of such activities keeps humanity's fragmentation strong in a way that runs much deeper than most of you are aware of at this time. Even individual body-wide movement or worship helps your own body function as a harmonious whole. Dancing, for instance, is good for all of you, both individually and collectively, and especially for those whose bodies may be falling apart. This is all. Be blessed.

11

The Earth:
The Fairy Kingdom, Dragon Power,
Creator Flow

The dragon and fairy kingdom is divided, as is all of nature, into four quadrants—that is, the flow from the center point of the Logos streams out in four directions. These four directions or divisions underlie all form in the universe. There are dragon forces committed to each of these four streams: red, green, gold, and black. There is also a hidden blue dragon, which brings special messages straight from the Logos center point itself and serves only God/Goddess. Each dragon lord or overlighting being of one of these streams has fairy or spirit forces at his command. These bring into all worlds the flow from the great center point in God's heart at the thirteenth Logos plane. This is accomplished via colored light or rays, which are gradually stepped down and coalesced into physical form on Earth, and is carried out with absolute love of and full surrender to the will of the Godhead, for such a combination will bring through the organizing principles with the highest level of perfection. All in dragon realms are very practiced in holding their own against the pressures of life and all wounding descent forces, and all have a strength of love that is as yet unknown in your world. The dragon forces are great teachers of such strengths, and indeed, when a seeker reaches the dragon levels, holding one's balance among fragmentation, pressure of all kinds, and deflection is one of the major teachings until mastery is achieved. It cannot be hurried. Once mastery has been stabilized, the great creator flow can begin.

This creator flow is the most powerful force in the cosmos and streams directly from the center point of God's Heart—the Beloved Christ's highest wishes and blessings—into the individual or vessel to be used in service and devotion to love within that world of form. The dragon kingdom is in full service to the creator energies and co-creates with God at the very highest and most powerful levels. We are Gods/Goddesses all, partners of Christ. In fact, any who reach this level in their unfoldment, the thirteenth plane of the Logos, are part of the dragon kingdom. There are representatives of them in all worlds.

In each of the four divisions—green, red, yellow, and black dragon kingdoms—all beings are paired with a single beloved partner. In fact, these two partners were created in one single flash of light, from one word spoken by the great Creator Sun. This sun is also a full union of God/Christ and Goddess/Magdalene, and all creations at every level were born out of their sacred sexual union within a full partnership based in equality, pleasure, delight, and desire. *Fairy* is simply another term for the devic/djinn forces of light beings that serve at all levels.

The dragon levels hold the secrets of the deep heart, the emotional drivers of all that happens in the universe. Emotion is the driving force of the All, and so the dragon guardians dole out rich and satisfying emotions from the deep heart of the Creator. The red dragon quadrant holds the emotions of passion, spice, and surprise. The green dragon quadrant holds those of desire, and giving and receiving love. The yellow dragon quadrant holds the emotions of the sovereignty of love, joy, victory, and glory. And the black dragon quadrant holds those of purity, intensity, intimacy, and union itself. We are honored to serve the Great Heart of Christ/Magdalene, King and Queen of Heaven, the Father/Mother's Kingdom of beloveds.

Each of these dragon guardian forces rules one of Earth's plant seasons as well as these emotional qualities. The shifts from one quadrant to another in the feminine emotional flow are marked by the high Celtic festivals of Imbolc on February 5, Beltane on May 5, Lughnasa on August 5, and Samhain during November 24 through 28. The red dragon stream comes into dominance at Imbolc, peaks at the vernal equinox, and diminishes at Beltane. Green dragon moves into dominance at Beltane, peaks at the summer solstice, and then wanes at Luhgnasa. Yellow dragon is dominant from Lughnasa to Samhain, peaking at the autumnal equinox. And black dragon is dominant from Samhain to Imbolc, peaking at midwinter. In truth, all dragon forces are active at all times, but one is more pronounced to drive the seasonal growth and activity.

Before we move into the descriptions of the four dragon kingdoms, we would like to make it very clear that male and female are held in absolute equality, sovereignty of self, respect of self and other, and full consideration of each other's wishes and desires. Love reigns here and no variance is allowed. It is a living choice and this entails the responsibility of holding the most intense emotions possible, with full and total surrender to the will of Magdalene/Christ. It is not an easy thing to do and demands long training and self-discipline. A great many try but do not achieve it. This was, in fact, the training of the Druid order and very few obtained the highest levels, where they could hold the creator flow within their grasp. Merlin was one. Jesus was another. The Druid and Kabbalistic paths are essentially the same. This will give you some idea of the quality of our devotion and the level of our powers.

All dragon energies are carried into Earth by the butterfly, moth, dragonfly, damselfly, insect, amphibian, fish, whale, arachnid, and reptilian forces. These are all fairies or devas and djinns in disguise. You could say they have on their insect suits in their physical form to cover their truth, but to any who observe spirit, it is clear they are winged ones of the realms of light. In fact, all kingdoms below mammalian hold reptilian or dragon tasks and easily go through the veil to choose their service for the day out of the many possibilities given by the will of God/Goddess. Each and every individual is included, for you are all tended closely and carefully by your guardian angels, who are in constant consultation with the Magdalene/Christ. The powers of all who spread dragon energies onto Earth are great and do not fail to have their chosen effect. One small intention sent on the wings of a butterfly with its soft and slowly opening path can quite easily change the entire planet. We give as our example the gentle love of Jesus, one man who lived two thousand years ago. The great force of his love has slowly and irrevocably transformed the face of the Earth. This is dragon power! You may wish to treat dragonflies, butterflies, insects, fish, and reptiles with more respect in the future, for nothing escapes their eyes, and they also choose the specific rebounding force for any misuse. These are intended as reminders of the Mother/Father's laws and not as punishment, as so many believe.

We would also like to state at the outset that our driving forces are open only to the use of pure love. We do not respond positively to any attempt to use our powers for money, for personal power, for fragmentation or destructive purposes of any kind. We serve love and love alone.

Like the Mother/Father's Kingdom, all dragon guardians live with their beloved, a single partner created with them, whose energies blend into the most blissful union possible. You would be amazed if you knew the depth of desire, devotion, and adoration we feel for each other in our eternal partnerships. Our scribe and very few others have achieved this level. She is just tasting the beginning of such a partnership after a long and arduous climb, and we applaud the gifts showering down from the Great Heart to one who is so deserving, despite her persistent feelings of unworthiness. With dragons around, darkness will not last too long!

Now, the four dragon kingdoms:

Red Dragon. The red dragon forces bring passion, surprise, and renewal. They can be found in red dragonflies, ladybugs, salamanders, some turtles, many fish, all red ants, and the *fritillaria* butterflies, especially the red and rose varieties. These forces are infused primarily into flowers, particularly pink and red varieties of roses. The fairy kingdom that serves this quadrant of the Great Heart is known as the fiona/finnegan forces. The devic or female ray color here is pink, and the djinn ray color is pepper red. If you could see the spirit form around a butterfly or dragonfly, you would see the fiona/finnegan themselves. These forces bring the energies primarily into roots and serve the little girl aspect of the Godhead, the fifth plane of the Logos and the east arm of the creator cross in the thirteenth plane. This little girl aspect is known as Michelle (my shell, the creator flame just behind the pubic bone, symbolized by a scallop shell) and her interests are the inner essence, transformation at the inner star level, and emergence of the authentic self. The element she oversees is air or spirit. The Celts would have called her Bride.

We of the red dragon spread the most intense passion, spiciness of life, sudden bursts of heart opening, surprise, and delight. We are absolute masters of keeping the veils covered until the very last moment and then whisking them away to a rushed opening of love— one of our special delights. These forces tend to be the smallest of physical forms, but as so often happens in spirit realms, the outer form disguises truth and our power is perhaps just a touch more than all the rest, for the Christ/Magdalene dearly love passion. Diminutive does not mean less powerful! Mark this well: To those who have achieved the dragon levels, messages will come or be asked for via our small forms. So, dear hearts all, if a red dragonfly or *fritillaria* land or hover near, stop for a moment and listen to her. She may want nothing more than to help deepen your passion for your beloved or his/her's for you! Delightful work! Red Dragon forms may also ask about deepening the fire in the heart for a particular cause or heart opening; this is the group that can and will set your heart on fire with love.

Green Dragon. The green dragon kingdom is dominant during summer and brings through the little boy aspect of the Great

Heart. The element these forces oversee is water. Their special province is manifestation of specific forms of love, or the giving and receiving of love in a certain form, one to another. Their own heart's desires, coming, of course, from the Magdalene/Christ, are to manifest your own deepest desires into specific forms of love. They will work tirelessly to achieve this. The essence of green dragon is the spurting exuberance of the little boy to connect with others and to engage in joyful play. He is known as Moss, or Cernunnos to the Celts, fourth plane of the Logos and western arm of the creator cross in the thirteenth Logos plane. His involvement brings juice to the mix. All plants are in service to this wish of The Great Heart, hence the predominant color of green in nature. Every green leaf and plant you see is devoted to bringing into manifestation your own specific heart's desires. Many plants, houseplants in particular, are readers of your deep heart energies and transmit these up to the Great Heart for inclusion into the creations of the future. If you bring the energies of red and green dragon together, you will have the truth of the universe. Every day is Christmas, full of sweet and loving surprises created just for you in love and love alone. Green dragon energies are carried by grasshoppers, frogs, leafhoppers, caterpillars, butterflies, moths, and nearly all whales and fish, especially the silver and green varieties. We are a widely varied group, some with rather slow building forces, and others with sudden rushes of love, either a giving or receiving force. We are those in charge of what you might call miracles and our forces are called the *sylvana* (devic)/*spiritus* (djinn) forces. We are particularly connected to trees and stalk, as in grasses, or in the juices of love, such as dew and sap. The divas and djinns of the *sylvana* are particularly full of desire for one another and co-create in the deepest bliss. The devic masters of this group are the feminine who organize and spread rays, and the masculine who hold to absolute truth or keep the axis centered. Our scribe and her beloved are of this order.

Gold Dragon. The third dragon kingdom, dominant in fall, is the gold dragon. This order disperses the regalness and sovereignty of love, the kingship and queenship of a particular realm that each being at this level chooses to be creator/steward over, as regent under God. It is a most elegant and powerful stream, for the gold dragon does not budge under fire; holding to the standard of love and love alone is this dragon's only desire. The force is a true rod of strength and is particularly evident in goldenrod. Gold dragon streams straight from the Father, eighth Logos plane and southern arm of the creator cross at the thirteenth Logos plane and comes through in flowers, stalks, butterflies (especially monarchs), shield bugs, mosquitoes, certain moths, snakes, and crickets. Yes, crickets will truly help with questions of conscience!

Fall is the time when activity is pulled back to center and the matchmaking tendencies of the Father become more evident, as couples prepare for the ingathering phase of winter. The golden dragon is full of snuggle and warm affection energies as the cold nights return. This is the teddy bear stream. If only you knew how very much like a teddy bear the Father in Heaven truly is! We of the golden dragon forces wish you only joy and love in your togetherness. The gold dragon forces are called the bees or hummers and serve primarily leaf and flower and some stalk, as in hay. We are very much a harvest-oriented group, helping with pollination, fruit, and yield, for the Great Hearted Father loves to give in abundance to his children. We are the soldiers of the dragon realm and will sting if you disturb sacred areas. We will also, as in the case of mosquitoes, carefully open your inner dragon lines with our bites and venom. This brings through so much more love for you! Our aim is perfect, and we are happy to serve. Once again, there is no such thing as *small* and *insignificant* in the dragon kingdom. The power of a tiny bug is equal in spiritual significance to that of the greatest elephant. We ask you to notice this and to respect both our powers and our ways, for all that we do is carefully designed to help you, though it may be disguised within an illusion of fear. Even the fears are carefully measured and precisely ordered to bring you into your full creatorhood. We hold and bless you in every moment. Be well.

Black Dragon. Last is the Mother's province, Her Womb, winter and Earth. Black dragon serves the first and seventh Logos planes and the northern arm of the creator cross in the thirteenth plane of the Logos. This essence comes in through stones, bones, oceans, and Earth depths. The Mother's is the bedrock essence, for She breaks down all old creations of the previous year and recycles them into pure potential for the creations of the year to come. She brings in the cosmic juices, the dark waters of Her Womb, which are primarily transformation essences. Hers is primarily a holding impulse, with comfort and healing as strong components. She will bring all into an affectionate embrace, one with another. She is even more snuggly than the Father! If only humanity knew the truth. Hers is also the province of mystery, for all that is to be revealed in the future comes from Her elemental Womb of endless and unlimited possibilities. Her other component is complete adoration and surrender to the organizing principles of the Father. She will do *anything* to see that His will is done and humanity served.

The forces and energies of the black dragon come primarily through snakes, turtles, black dragonflies, spiders, toads, and, much less strongly, through moths, butterflies, and insects. Until fear illusions are cleared, the Mother's focus is in bringing these to the attention of the seeker. After the clearing work is complete, Her focus will be to bring forth the deepest and most all encompassing desires.

Her energies and power are dominant on Earth, and the suffering She has undergone to bring all of you into your full, separate identity consciousness is great. She is truly the Queen of both Heaven and Earth. She is the object of devoted adoration in all realms, and happy will be the day when humanity releases itself from fear and comes to understand and revere and heal Her—body, mind, soul, and spirit. Her mastery at all levels—mind, heart, body, soul, and spirit—knows no parallel. We of spirit realms long for Her full freedom from pain.

There is one dragon force working with silent swiftness who may be less obvious than the rest. **The Blue Dragon** serves the third Logos plane and does not belong with the four previous dragon kingdoms, but comes when great speed or mercy are required. This is the blue or silver-blue dragon, coming through in small butterflies and dragonflies in particular, many of whom are endangered in these times. They carry important messages from the Christ to all seekers who are in especial pain or when the need is great. So, if you see a blue-white dragonfly hovering about, be sure to stop and listen well. It may bring a message that will heal or lead you with a gentle intensity unknown to the other groups.

Our scribe has asked us to clear the confusion as to where angelic realms may fit with fairy realms. We have not included the angelic kingdom here, for they are not of the Celtic system but belong more closely to the Father's realm of Heaven. The Otherworld of the Mother is the land of spirit forces connected with manifestation on Earth, so all are intimately connected with this world, though they can and do travel easily from realm to realm. The fairy or devic/djinn kingdom is all around you; the fairies never left. Once on Earth, both spirit and body were joined and became one. The Mother's kingdom, the Celtic realm, is the spirit realm of Earth and is fully grounded in this plane of manifestation.

The angelic realms are primarily celestial and live at the Paradisiacal levels, though in their work they also can and do travel to any plane. They come here to assist, and two or more are assigned by the Father as guardians through every human life to each human being. But they are not of Earth and must often do their work through those of the devic/djinn kingdoms, who are versed in working with the physical, as angels are not. The devic, djinn, and angelic realms work very closely with one another, but the devic serves the Mother and the djinn and angelic serve the Father.

We of the devic/djinn realms would like simply to add that we are your family in every way and you will someday remember the close connections we had with you before the veil closed. Our love for you is great and very deep is our sorrow at the distance between us. We ache to bridge these divisions and to heal you, for this also heals us. We will work in any endeavor with any and all who hold love and peace in their hearts. We are particularly gifted in transformation through ritual, as you will all soon discover. Be blessed and held in the tender love of Christ/Magdalene each and every moment of your lives.

Our scribe has a heart's desire we are choosing to bring to the fore now and it is this: to establish a community on the Isle of Skye in Scotland, her motherland, where every inner child's deep heart can come into complete healing and open the door for a union of the fairy and human kingdoms once more. She is deeply committed to making this a living reality and asks for support and committed companions who wish to join her and her beloved in this ambitious and generous task. Her heart energies are particularly attuned to healing the deep heart wounds of the inner child, and a healing center and teaching facility would be most important, as would others who share her understanding of and willingness to live according to the Mother/Father's laws. We wish her well in her chosen destiny. We of the fairy realms wish to state that hers is a gentle heart, fierce in its love of the child and its surrender to Christ. She is one of very few humans on the planet who would have our full cooperation in her endeavor.

Those who have not done the inner clearing work be forewarned that all of fairy are in service to love and love alone. If anyone attempts to force or coerce us for any other purpose, this in turn forces us to send them reminders that they are not aligned with the highest levels and the greater good. This is a direct teaching method of the Christ/Magdalene and one we fully support. So, those who experience shifting energies or negative surprises from nature: Instead of hurting us, look instead inside yourselves to determine the true reason for such a message. All that we do is fully anchored in service to love and love alone.

A word of caution: There are methods of magic now in use around the planet that can and will open the soul or spirit powerfully and quickly. We wish to state firmly that all such intense and rapid shifts in consciousness are ultimately harmful to the spirit, which is a delicate and gentle life, and we do not support them. Only gradual and gentle methods of change are supported by spirit realms. Because of your independence and your creator powers, we do come in and work with you, but those who attempt to climb too fast will learn in time the difficulties of such methods. We simply ask you to consider the gentleness of the inner spirit in your choices.

One more word of caution: Please be careful in making contracts about what to believe; consider carefully who and what powers you believe in, for it is these contracts and beliefs that in the end create the outer reality of your world. Whenever someone wishes you to connect and agree to something not based in love, you are essentially contracting to believe in a false love stream at that level. Hold the highest level of expectation for yourselves at all times! Speak out when what is happening is not occurring in love! You would be truly amazed at the power of these two points of focus alone to diminish evil in your world, and at the rapidity of changes this would bring about.

❧12❧
The Arthurian Promise:
The Fulfillment, Bird

This final chapter gives you the revelation of the final mystery of humanity. Like all acts of God, it is simple, yet full of grace and the powerful purity of homey love.

Each person was created in wholeness and perfection in one instant. God had the thought of her or him and, voilà, in less than a second that person was standing there. Actually, each person was created as part of a pair. In every instance, not one, but two beings were created. These two belong together. Their natures blend so perfectly that it is as though they were held in union within the Heart of God before being brought forth from it into individuality. Each is the only one in the cosmos who can bring this experience of full union to the other. And once they meet there is no stopping it, for their hearts and natures are so deeply connected, union becomes inevitable.

However, this journey to union is never easy. There are obstacles you must meet and transform along the way. It is necessary to face and clear many, many fears before this opening occurs. Your connection to the Source of love must be cleared of fear-based illusions, personality issues, archetypal stereotypes, and false gods. Along the way to this enlightenment there are false beloveds and great isolation. So, your discrimination becomes quite fine-tuned. Mastery of your own sexual creator powers is learned. Disappointment and discouragement crop up along the way. And even when the one you have been waited for appears, he or she will come in disguise; they will not be what you have remembered or hoped for. The veils must be removed little by little, and slowly the memories come. Love opens her petals gradually. There is great humor, burning desire, heartbreaking discouragement, deep inner insecurity, and miraculous surprise. This courtship is a slow and steady one, for there is none other like it. In pure delight, God returns you to Him/Herself with this courtship. Gradually, trust grows and security comes, as do passionate sensuality and the homely comfort of best friends. Even if each of you do not consciously remember being together in some capacity in every lifetime and in every form you have assumed, your heart will feel this depth, the deep knowing of the other all the way back to the beginning.

It is a love like no other. And it is God restored to you. For He/She is the Source of Love who created and carried you through every moment of your descent and holds you, even now, even in your darkest hour, with a purity and passion of love that you who live in fear cannot imagine. Only this one beloved, created for this purpose in particular, can bring you to this experience. In truth, God is your best friend, your lover, your everything, for all you see and feel and touch is one with His/Her body. There is nothing outside of God. It is the depth of love He/She feels that God wishes to show you in this one beloved. It is the height of love and very, very few have so far attained it. It is to this end that the clearing work is done and all the hardships and pain are endured.

When each of you has cleared your inner channels of light all the way up to the center point of the Source of love, the Godhead, then the time of the fulfillment will come. In the opening of love, each of you will know the fullness and will feel loved as a god or goddess. In the sexual union of such beloveds, the symbols of light that organize your yearly outer experience, and that are implanted into everyone on midwinter morning, will descend straight from the nucleus of the Godhead through the male form and into the female form and be implanted there in the womb. These will manifest each partner's deepest heart's desires and it will be obvious that together you are creators of your manifested reality. And you are. These are your powers. You were created in the full image of God. This is precisely how all worlds and all forms were and are created, in a pure and passionate sexual co-creative union of the male and female aspects of God within their various forms.

There was one more reason for your descent: your sensuality. The Godhead is a spirit form, spirit, becoming without end. As spirit, it is made of light, only light, nothing more. The male is sun, the female a different form of sun, with light very much like your reflective moon, but it is an inner light, not reflected at all. And when they co-create, these suns come together and sparks fly—many stars are born. It is how you and the partner created for you were brought forth before the beginning of time.

In Heaven there is only light, no flesh. You asked to be made into physical beings so that when you came together in union, you could feel this in flesh; you could hug and hold as those in the spirit world cannot do. It is a great gift and blessing. For this your light had to be slowed, frozen in fact. The physical body is frozen light, with the soul and spirit inside to keep it moving so that it will not freeze completely.

To slow down light, a great deal of fear had to be created—so much fear. Nightmare after nightmare was lived through, until the spirit closed itself off and shut down and left the Father's Kingdom with the Mother. Her light and yours together make a soul substance that is more watery than spirit, as water is to steam. Then more fears came, more and more and more, until the children of God left even the Mother's realm and came finally into flesh. The Father's spirit still was hidden within you, and the soul of the Mother was within everyone—otherwise, your flesh would be like ice. You wouldn't be able to move a bit. Your physical-soul-spirit form is an incredible miracle of creation that has been eons and eons in the making. It is a gift of the very highest order, as are all the physical forms of plants and animals surrounding you, for they volunteered to live through the nightmares to be with you. They have held all the pieces of your soul (animals) and spirit (plants) you left behind, waiting to restore them to you as you ascend.

And most important, Your Divine Mother descended with you. She just could not bear to have you gone, so She disguised Herself as Earth and covered Her beautiful lunar sun with soil and sea to keep Herself secret from you so that you could forget everything. It was necessary to forget to become truly independent in your mind, heart, and body. But it is time now for you to remember both yourselves and Her. She longs and waits for you to turn to Her and share again the love you once knew. She weeps for all who are in pain and would help all of you. Her life is poured out for you in nature, in water, in the air you breath. Her presence and Her great love for each of you are in all of it.

When you hurt nature, you are hurting Her, causing great suffering and great pain to the One who loves you so deeply. She asked to undergo all that you yourselves have to suffer, for only one who lives this pain can have enough compassion to hold and to heal it, and this is Her great gift to you. She has carried and supported you in every way through all your lives. She knows you thoroughly and understands your every pain. She understands your wish to violate and harm and lash out in your extremity of suffering because She has heard and held and seen it all. She knows how hard it's been. She knows. She did all this to hold you especially on your return, because only Her great love and understanding could bring enough compassion to bear truly to heal you.

It was Her heart that was entrusted to the one you call Jesus. His form was male because he was sent from the Father, who holds Heaven together, waiting for all the lost ones to return. But it was *the Mother's heart* that Jesus carried inside him. And all of you are no different. You left your Father's realm to suffer here along with Her to keep compassion and the wisdom of the Godhead renewed and alive, for God is living and renewal is sometimes required. You have suffered full measure in pure service to Her, and the physical form is Her exquisite gift to each of you. When you eat and drink and see and touch, it is Her body you take in, all of it, every living thing. It is a living gift of love from Her to you in all your suffering. There is much sweetness here. Mark it well and open to the knowing, for it will intoxicate and delight you.

The fulfillment is the gift of your Father and is of His design. For the eons of separation, loneliness, and insecurity you have endured to create individual identity that preserves and refreshes Him, He chose a pure, holy, and passionate partner for each of you. And He chose an absolute security of love, beyond all others, to which to return. And when your clearing work is done, this love that comes straight from Him, from highest Heaven, will appear. For Heaven is the God who is your own Beloved, who creates each petal, each breath, every hair, just for you. His passion and purity of love know no bounds. In your true beloved, it is His own love coming through to you.

So there you are, the full human-spirit blend. Your great gifts are deep compassion for all pain, deep wisdom born of hard experience, the knowledge of all others as the Body of Your Mother, the exquisite pleasure of the physical, a pure and passionate love for one intimate beloved, and the strength and empowerment of your own individual identity based in truth and love. These are your eternal gifts in grace for all the painful service you have offered. May all bring you bountiful pleasure, great joy and bliss, and, of course, ever more love. Be blessed.

We must speak to you of your return, for it is a difficult climb that may take many, many lifetimes, for every fear belief you learned on the way down must be faced in love and vanquished. It is not easy. There are four basic levels of ascension: those of personality, soul, spirit, and Logos. To any who are truly committed and set their heart's toward good, the way will be made clear, and both the natural and spirit worlds will hold these individuals in protection—for as the inner spirit creator powers open, fear beliefs are created outside in quite an accelerated fashion. We would refer you to our scribe's book *The Lost Star Children of Ur (Earth),* for in it the clearing method and the steps on the way are described in full detail. This is not our task here. We simply wish to help you on your way, you who remain enclosed in the thick casing of fear and do not feel God and do not feel love.

Here we clear some of the most common confusions for you, to help you on your way:

1. God loves you. He/She is not a sadistic or powerful over-lord who wants to control, dominate, or harm you. All such beliefs are illusions taken in during your times of descent. God is a Gentle Heart, like Jesus, who sends Himself over and over into your world to sustain horrible wounds and even to die to get the message of love to you and bring you Home.

2. Your God is not a distant detached superior being, who inhabits a far off star system or world in another realm. Your God is the creator of all worlds and all things and all are a part of His/Her Body. You are part of His/Her Body. Your God lives within and without and all around you. He/She has never left you and never will and is intimately involved in every aspect of your life.

3. Your God is not a hateful parent who threw you overboard into the great abyss or banished you from Heaven. Your God is a master of creativity who created all experiences, including fears, to follow the route you yourselves chose and desired to take. All has been created to give you your-self precisely what you asked for. This is the most basic

truth about God. He/She adores filling heart's desires in delightful, magical, and surprising ways.

4. Your God is not a maniacal demon, who likes power or money and who creates through darkness and fragmentation. He/She is the most tender and gentle Spirit imaginable, loving each of you with a purity and passion that keeps you alive and taking note of every breath. Yes, every hair is counted, and you are held so dearly and lovingly in that Great Heart. If only you could feel this now!

5. Your God is not a wicked stepmother who wants to be prettier and more powerful than you and who will steal and destroy your power. Your True Mother holds and nourishes you in every moment. Your body is lovingly made out of Her Own Body, so She literally holds, carries, and loves you in every moment. All pain that you feel, She feels, too. This is absolutely true.

6. Your God is not a sexual pervert who wants to rape or sodomize you or close down and use your creator powers for personal gain. He/She wishes to gently, but as swiftly as may be, empower you to face your many fears and release you from the chains of evil binding you. His/Her heart aches to bring you all into freedom and love once more. It is His/Her greatest desire and will.

7. Your God does not want you to sacrifice yourself or anyone else to Him/Her in any way. He/She wants you to follow your heart, do what you truly love, and learn that this is the only way to freedom.

8. Your God does not want to use you to work, work, work, and work some more for His/Her glory or purposes. He/She does not want you to race, rush, or hurry in any way. He/She wants you to make a firm commitment to

grow in love and to find a path to embody gradually Him/Her—not out of pride or dominance but instead stemming purely from the aching wish to bring you Home and back to love.

9. Your God does not enjoy seeing you suffer or endure pain of any kind. His/Her heart quivers in sadness whenever this occurs and waits for your call for aid in your empowerment phase. All is done to create a you in light, as you yourselves requested. These painful layers of growth transform you into your full divinity and each is necessary. It is an exquisitely beautiful plan and, in time, all will see and feel deep awe and gratitude for it. We hope this day comes soon. The spirit world is working overtime, now that the cycle has shifted, to bring you out of suffering and into love and light as swiftly as may be.

10. You are not innately an evil sinner who can never be redeemed for what you may have done, perhaps, horrific actions based in fear. You are a child of God, made precisely in His/Her image, who is a very long way from Home and has been carrying a severe load of suffering and oblivion and doing the very best you can. The spirit world is well aware of all the wounds you have sustained and the severity of extremes you often live within.

We are truly amazed at you and cannot imagine enduring what you often go through. We sometimes send uplifting messages, but they don't register because we don't experience what you do. Please forgive us. It is all we know to do. We do have great wisdom and sound advice from having helped so many in their climb to salvation and release from bondage to fear. We are masters in that work and can and will resolve any and all confusions for you. We surround you and send you our purest love every moment, hoping to get through to each of you. This effort is doubled or tripled when you call. It does help us when you consciously open a pathway for us through guided imagery or music, which can easily move through your barriers. We hold and bless you on your way.

THE BIRD KINGDOM

These are the totem birds of the Celtic realms, birds most known and worked with by the druid priests and priestesses. These birds have become most linked with the Celtic path of return, but all birds will work with any human and at any level; there are no hard and fast rules.

We begin with crow and raven, the birds of the soul at the lower gateway to soul realms, and swan at the upper gateway into spirit realms. Then we move to birds of the spirit realms: Grebe and Goldfinch. Grebe is located at the lower entrance to spirit levels and Goldfinch at the upper entrance to the Logos. From their planes the birds listed are linked directly with the ray lords of the Logos planes. Crows will also travel to the Logos at the wisdom or first plane. The falcon is of the second Logos plane or the Elohim; starlings are from the third Logos plane, the river of life. These are followed by the cardinal of the boy of the fourth Logos plane and the chickadee and bluebird of the little girl of the fifth Logos plane. Owls stream from the sixth Logos plane, the Arthurian realm; the hummingbird streams from the Mother's sky realm, or the seventh Logos plane. They are followed by the hawk of the Father's realm, the eighth Logos plane. Robins hold the three-in-one wholeness stream of the ninth Logos plane, while the four dragon arms of the creator cross in the thirteenth plane are represented by the sparrow and the kingfisher of the boy aspect, the eagle of the father aspect, the wren of the little girl, and the goose of the mother. The creators at the fourteenth Logos plane are brought through by the jay and the cardinal of the male creator and the peacock of the female creator. (We have not included the peacock as it was never a bird common to the Celtic path.)

The bird kingdom is dedicated entirely to bringing through the

Arthurian fulfillment. In the Celtic system, there is one bird for each of the one hundred and twenty-eight planes of form, and the twelve aspects of the Godhead—one hundred forty in all. Each bird is easily capable of moving from one dimension to another and does so regularly. They bring messages back and forth and are attendants for the ray lords of each level. The bird kingdom is committed to carrying messages back and forth, to move forward the mission and purpose of the planes they descend from. It is too complicated a system to elucidate fully here. We will explain the most common and powerful birds now working with you. These birds were all well-known and befriended by druid masters from long ago into the present.

Druid Birds

1. Crow/Raven. This is the bird of the soul. It carries the soul through the veil when it leaves the physical body, and these birds are the guardians of the path of return. They know the way and can lead you on your path Home. These birds are masters of spirit realms and can guide you through wrong turns or slippery spirit demons who pose as love. They are eager to work with you. They are peace loving, but the strongest of warriors, and will go into the deepest darkness to save a soul. Crows are in service to wisdom or the Mother. Ravens are in service to the full return to sovereignty of the Father or Christ, the King.

2. Swan. The swan is the bird signifying the grace and sovereignty of the divine feminine. Swans descend from the Mother in the Godhead. She will lead you into complete healing of your fallen feminine and will bring you safely to truth, beauty, and the entrance to the Father's realm when the spirit opens and the child of light emerges. She is a particular master of negotiating the most difficult trials of the soul assent. She can and often does energetically come in beneath you to physically lift you to the next level when you are trying but still remain stuck. She will fiercely stand by any pilgrim until death. Her commitment is complete and intense, as is that of the Mother from which she streams. She can and does carry messages directly to the Mother or to the Christ. If you feel your prayers are not getting through, see the swan. She will be a strong adversary for you.

3. Grebe. The grebe is a bird of the shore and, like most shore birds, it holds memories of paradise. It will help you see how miraculous and lovely are even the most ordinary of experiences, such as a morning breeze, a walk in the sand. It has a homely and deeply loving character, full of uniqueness—even eccentricity—and independence, mixed with the wish to hold and love each of you in your particular gifts. It will see you as a totally adorable child of God and can help you remember yourself that way. The grebe is a particularly happy bird.

4. Finch. The finches are closely connected to the Mother's peace and the balance that occurs when She returns at dusk, a calming down at the end of the day. All finches have a sensitivity to noise and sudden movement that makes them shy and easily startled. Goldfinches are especially aligned with the Father and His matchmaking tendencies. They will always be found in pairs and share the highest and truest love. They keep to themselves and hold this beloved intimacy stream. When goldfinches are nearby, your Beloved God is hovering there, too, asking you to come and be His/Her love for just a while. His/Her heart is bursting for some release of love to you. These birds precede pure grace.

5. Falcon. The Falcon is the harpooner bird. It sends into the seeker's heart a direct stream of the wild love of Christ that plunges straight from great heights into the depths. It has a sharp eye for purity of purpose, planting precise and personal messages there to ripen and bear the fruit of spiritual love. This bird connects directly to the right heart. It knows the places of especial holiness and wildness in every area of your planet, where space for the eternal Earth is still being held, and will lead to these ancient places all seekers who come in love and need of transformation. This bird's purpose is very closely connected to the druid's as well.

6. Starling. Starlings are the bird of groups. They teach how all groups are truly one and that if all group members were aware, they would see that they operate as a single consciousness, a single will, and how each individual heart is just as necessary to the full unfoldment of the group as every other. Starlings will help you get over your separation shyness and your shame about being seen in a group. They can help you learn to be your own self, just as you are, and to share in giving and receiving in a balanced and natural way. These birds know the soaring that comes within the natural flow of a group effort. Starlings are the bird of the new millennium.

7. Cardinal, Royal Bird. Cardinals are the thrusting bird. They will take a direction for an individual straight from the Heart of God and push its power, grace, and beauty perfectly into the heart of the one for whom that dream was created. They are invincible and impossibly determined birds; nothing can stand in their way. They are emissaries of pure grace and teachings from on high. These birds are in service to the Father and are always chosen when need is great and speed is required. There are no birds in all Christendom who will go to greater lengths to serve the will of Christ. It is a glorious bird.

8. Bluebird. The bluebird is a most happy bird and will come to bring you peace and passionate uplifting whenever you are particularly low. It has a stream of irrepressible joy to give you and will find a humorous way to break your blues with its antics or funny faces. It is very connected to the inner child and the sentiment of "zippity-do-da, my, oh my, what a wonderful day!" It is also quite determined in its joy and will find a way to reach you. It has a particularly wild sense of humor.

9. Chickadee. Chickadees are of the delicate butterfly nature, that of the inner girl. They are chattery and into everything and are curious and most happy. These birds are particularly bright in spirit and are connected to happy outcomes. They will come and cheer you in the dark nights of the soul, telling you that all is well and that you will break free before too long. Having an inner lamp of the heart and mind that simply refuses to go out, they are the bird of optimism and singing in the rain.

10. Owl. Owls are priest birds. They bring holiness and mystery of the highest order, connecting to the most ancient wisdom of the eternal realms, and will help you decipher ancient secrets and ancient languages or symbols of any kind. The owl is the bird most closely connected with transformation. If owls come to you, you are about to light up with God! These birds are not to be tampered with or harmed, for their connections with the priests and priestesses of the Otherworld bring the deepest and most powerful agents for change and uplifting into Earth. Extinction will occur at your peril—beware. This is the druid bird.

11. Hummingbird. The hummingbird is the quintessential bird of the Mother's realm. It is a freedom-loving bird and will never succumb to domination or captivity of any kind. It would rather lose its life than its freedom. It feeds from the nectar of the Mother, food of Heaven, made from the closest communion of flowers and the Christ/Magdalene creators in pure and passionate union. This keeps hummingbirds pure and joyful. Female hummingbirds are especially excellent mothers and will give their last breath to care for their young. Any visitation from a hummingbird is an unusual event, for these are shy and reclusive birds, and is certainly a message from the Mother that freedom is near or that it is a heavenly day to come and enjoy with Her Paradisiacal streams to flood your mind and heart straight from Hers.

12. Hawk. The hawk is the bird of direct purpose. It will show and teach you how to follow single-minded focus and intention into full manifestation of will. It is the bird of willpower aligned with spirit—with this combination, there is nothing that can stand in its way. It is a most determined bird, committed to the full flowering of identity.

13. Robin. The robin is the family bird, the holy family. It embodies and can show all the way to gentle, loving harmony within the family fold. It is fully committed to the inner child especially and, like a good family member, will listen and hold all a person wants to tell it, particularly their wounds or when they've had a hard day. It embodies the Divine Child nature and is fully in service to bearing the wounds of family and parent and standing in a gentle, loving kindness that silently holds and heals in the most powerful and unseen way. These birds hold the hominess of God all around you, in ordinary ways you might not even notice if you are unaware. Robins are very connected to dogs, that aspect of God that wishes to be your best friend, and will do their best to comfort and uplift you through thick and thin. The Robin's song goes straight to the deep Divine Child heart and opens it.

14. Sparrow. The Sparrow is a holy bird, connected to the Divine Child who fell, the boy or cherub with a broken wing who is lost in this world of fear. Like the fallen children of God who are all around you, sparrows are everywhere. They are experts at making the best out of a bad situation, finding a compromised space and making it homey and comfortable, and singing out in love all the livelong day, no matter what is wrong. Their natures are particularly gentle and kind and do not waiver in the face of a storm. They work very closely with particular individuals and their song goes straight to the deep heart, to calm and comfort it and remind it of Home.

15. Kingfisher, Royal Bird. The kingfisher is the depths-diving bird. It is the bringer of pure light, those strong shafts that can penetrate to the very depths of darkness to release the wisdom held captive there. The kingfisher's commitment is to the wounds of the sovereigns within, the inner rulers, both male and female. For it is only this partnership, both male and female held in balance, that can truly rule in love. This bird brings light, strong and secure, directly from the throne of Christ, the diamond light of love from the center point. This light can reach through any and all darkness to open or implant the seeds of truth that disperse and dissolve fear. The kingfisher is the freedom bird!

16. Eagle, Royal Bird. The eagle is the bird of the Father's Kingdom. It holds the highest view. It can see and integrate what is happening from the highest levels, and it will bring such insights to you. It is fully committed to the Arthurian fulfillment and is a guardian and protector of righteousness, especially for women and children. It embodies the chivalric code and the purity of the divine masculine, and is an unparalleled champion of truth and justice. It is no accident this bird is the emblem of the United States or that its shape is also that of the sacred Scottish Isle of Iona. Both places hold memories of the beloved levels and can and will bring you to your fulfillment phase. It is a most heartily strong and joyful bird.

17. Wren, Royal Bird. The wren is the harbinger of spring. It is connected to the inner girl, with a small and delicate butterfly nature that is shy of roughness and totally independent. This bird's delicacy is most powerful; indeed, this tiny creature is one of the most powerful in the bird kingdom. It connects to the Pleiades, the unborn seven generations to come, waves of the future, and holds the softness of newborn babies. It brings with these newborn streams a freshness and new growth for the Earth, the new life and rejuvenation so closely connected to spring. If you see the wren, spring or some kind of rejuvenation in your life is never far behind.

18. Goose, Royal Bird. This is the Celtic bird that signifies the Holy Spirit. The Canadian or arctic goose in particular is the bird of the Divine Father and Mother. These birds show you how your True Mother and Father God will fly extreme distances to bring you Home. These birds work very individually with particular people and the trees of each of these individuals and will fight to the death or take on extreme wounds to complete their work and get through to you. They are again connected to the inner child who feels abandoned and lost. Their presence signifies that your Divine Mother and Father are nearby and watching over you. Geese are particularly connected to the

Mother's concern for easing pain, especially heartache—it is a most holy and protective bird. Like swans, geese often place their etheric bodies beneath you to help you rise to your next level through the birth pressure that comes with each passage from one plane to another. They are also linked to midwives and the process of rebirth. These are the guardian birds, particular defenders of the child against dark spirits.

19. Jay, Royal Bird. The jay comes from the center point of the Godhead. It carries nuclear light symbols and is particularly attendant on those working at the beloved levels, for these pilgrims are changing their DNA. It is a master of swiftness in action with one pointed focus, and of taking an assertive stance of absolute truth in the face of any and all darkness. The jay is a fierce warrior and ally. Its work is particularly important and intense on midwinter morning.

The bird kingdom wishes to thank you for your enduring contribution of sacrifice and suffering to renew the wisdom stream. Only the most courageous spirits volunteer to carry this shroud and transform through it back again to Home. We wish you to know you are tenderly loved by us all. We carefully watch over you and have a closely knit global network that can bring messages or help from far away across the planet or from the highest realms. We are, in particular, the messengers of prayer and deliver these wishes, blessings, and requests to the throne room of Christ, the King. We are often the messengers that take His grace to the one prayed for and deliver His wishes to the nature kingdom to perform. Our work is tireless and we can create the tiniest uplifting influences to keep you faith-filled and bring you Home. If you see a surprise of nature, such as a particular juxtaposition of flowers, a butterfly that comes near you, or sunset radiance, it is the word of our winged warriors that have sent the cry for help and brought down Christ's response, which has been so tenderly created for you. We are in every way your allies and will be with you until the end. Our hearts want nothing more than true love for each and every one of you. We love you more than we can say.

We would like to ask you to become more aware of us and our workings, for these conscious connections can bring our work much more powerfully to you. We would also like to state that the small surprises you see and feel, nature's delicacies, the synchronicities of life, even unusually timed phone calls, are all a result of the work of the global bird family. Each time one of these occurs, one of us has been watching you, feeling and holding your pain, and has flown to Heaven to make requests for you. And then another one of us—or the same one—has carried Christ's particular solution to that pain, a gift from Him tenderly created and handed out just for you, and has given His instructions to the djinns and divas, the male and female regents of creativity, so that they can perform it. There are many forces at work to serve and help you, and our hearts and minds hold only love. It is the sweet love of God we bring to our service and we would have you know and experience us this way now.

In particular, because we are the instruments of prayer, it would be most helpful to call in the bird kingdom when you pray, especially when you need a sign to resolve a pain or confusion. We particularly love to work with song, so all those songs you hear on the radio in answer to prayers come from us. We love this work.

Our most delightful joy is to carry messages back and forth between you and the one beloved created for you. We are most adept at this and will spare nothing to get through. Some of the war challenges in this regard were particularly intense, and many of our numbers, like yours, were lost and were quickly replaced by others until the fight was won. We will bring you thoughts and memories of your beloved, as long as Christ approves the timing and the union. We are the group that knows the most about opening love-lost hearts who are in despair and who are hopeless of ever finding love that's true. This is our most precious service to mankind, and we will sing you the songs of love and the beloved until our dying day and beyond. Because of this, we would ask you to please reduce your use of pesticides, or to at least consciously ask us if they are safe for use, for we are dying by the thousands. Even so, like you, we will persist in fighting the good fight and serving until the Father's Kingdom manifests in every heart, in every life, here on Earth. We kneel before the Christ/Magdalene's Great Heart and Love, and we give in wide and full array to the dawning of that day. Hurrah!

{13}

Our Wish for You

Nature longs to reach out to each and every one of you. We remember you individually from your spiritual birth and childhood, before your spirit closed during your descent. We were your closest friends and allies and we held, spoke, played with, and delighted you. It was such a wonderful surprise to see you grow and change and to evolve ourselves. We have lived with you in every world of your descent and know you intimately, much of the time better than you know yourselves.

We are particularly eager to reconnect with the child spirits we once knew, to hold hands, to gaze at you, full of love, to giggle with you in the forest. Most particularly, we wish to help you slow down and learn to *be* again, in silent joy and closeness—and, of course, most of all, we wish to help you to play! You see, we do remember you, the spirit child in you all. We know what your child needs to feel safe and secure, to heal and to unfold into the safety and security of love's fulfillment once more. We listen to your thoughts and feel your many heart's desires, and we love you. We ache to connect consciously and co-create with you, to fill the loving wishes of your True Father and Mother, and, once the healing of fear has occurred, to fulfill your heart's desires magnificently. You who have suffered so very much have only the faintest glimmer of the wonder and delights in store for you once your clearing work is complete.

We, too, have been evolving in these eons of separation and we have honed the fireworks of our imaginations to bring to you wild surprise, the most mysterious holiness, the broadest support we can create, and ordinary moments so full of the One Beloved's sweetness. Some of you, like our scribe and a few others, are beginning to tap these treasures. For all who still flounder in pain, we ask you especially to take our hands, take the Mother's hand and heart, and let us come to you and hold you and bring you through the trials and pain you still must endure to break free. Let us all work together to see you through, with strength of heart, courage of spirit, and love that endures all things and eternally prevails.

In this sacred work, let us forge a new alliance in love, the partnership of Beloved to beloved, as spirits knowing only truth and the eternal light of grace and beauty. Let us hold the torch of love higher and burning ever brighter in simple joyful partnership. Let us take comfort time together, for you do not know how it uplifts us to see you smile, to see your hearts relax, and know we are getting through. If only you could hear our telepathic hurrahs. It brightens us, too. There are wonders we could do together, magnificent possibilities that remain unformed.

We would especially ask you to bring us your broken children, the inner children in all adults, the elderly, the homeless, the disabled, the sick, the grieving, the impoverished, the tormented, the refugees living in such extremes of non-love. We know how to heal their pain and we ache for work like this. We long to bring those so terribly broken into the province of our hearts and bodies that hold only love. We long for the clearing work to be complete, so that we are no longer forced to reflect your fears to you, when all can break free into the grand and glorious celebration of love that awaits humanity. We say hurrah to all of you weary spirit warriors of love. We support you and hold you and ache so deeply to bring you home, everyone. So be it. Soon. Hurrah we say and again to our friends and human family, hurrah!

Our scribe has requested, and we fully agree, to end with deep reverence and gratitude to Christ/Magdalene, the One Beloved of all, the Great Heart holding true and enduring love for each and every one. It is proper to do so. So, let us all kneel, the world around and worlds above, for one moment of solemn and thankful prayer.

To you, our Christ/Magdalene Redeemer, who leads us all to higher and higher forms of love and love's experience, we gratefully offer thanks and honor. We dedicate our whole hearts, our complete minds, and the full force of our life's power to serving you, your Heart, your Love. We vow to bring your miraculous saving grace through to any and all in need, to work tirelessly for the full healing of every heart and every pain, and all disease in humanity and in nature across this glorious and exquisitely beautiful planet you have made and entrusted to us. We vow now to come into full brotherhood and conscious union with each other and with you, toward the anchoring in of your precious and glorious Kingdom onto Earth, that the fullness of the beauty and tender compassion of your heart may finally be revealed. So be it. Amen.

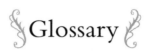

Glossary

androgyne: Boy and girl spirit fused; the Divine Child.

Brigid: Celtic Mother Goddess, same as Mother Mary.

clairaudience: The ability to hear messages from spirit realms.

devic: Having to do with devas or djinns.

focalize: To bring rays through the heart for a specific purpose.

the fulfillment: The everlasting partnership between two individuated spirit-soul-persons who were originally created together. The possibilities for physical, soul, and spirit expression of love within such a partnership knows no bounds.

impunity: Without harm.

inviolable: Not to be violated or broken.

Iona: Goddess who holds within stone and bone all memories of fear and love from spirit realms; the Earth Mother who guards the sanctity and purity of light on Earth. It is She who brings forward the opposing forces and fear memories for clearing, reopens the memories and embodiment of light or love, and builds the child of light or the divinity of each human on their ascension path.

Jerusalem: Goddess of Liberty, consort of the Father in Heaven, Mother of all who descended into individuation and full separate consciousness; warrior Goddess who holds the pole of light consciousness on Earth against all evil and for all time; Woman clothed with the Sun. She streams from the dragon kingdom plane of the Logos and rules the place of rest, refreshment, and bliss, where all wounds are healed and refabricated into a consciousness of love alone, and where evolving souls live after their time in lower worlds.

Julian–Gregorian Calendar: Annual calendar set up by Roman law. It follows the twelve-month, thirty-day cycle of the Father in Heaven.

Magdalene: Bride of Christ, Queen of Heaven, Mother of All who descended into darkness with Her children and holds the pole of light in darkness for the cosmic feminine for all worlds; the Feminine Creator who brings the creator stream into Earth for manifestation of light into all forms; the Womb or Cosmic Mother who has the power to break down and reform any and all forms into pure potentiality. She streams from the center point of the Logos.

Mother Mary: Mary is the body of humanity, which is collectively birthing the Christ/Magdalene incarnate on Earth. The overlighting Goddess of the feminine aspect of all humans on Earth no matter which gender they are currently playing out.

phoenix: Egyptian mythical bird who lived for five hundred years, was destroyed by fire, and rose from the ashes of its own destruction again and again; a symbol of immortality.

tarantella: Whirling southern Italian dance for couples.

thymus gland: Located between heart and throat in the upper chest, it is connected to immune function of the body. It radiates the healing love of the Divine Child and sinks into the second chakra at puberty, when this inner child is closed down and hidden. It can be opened and raised through spiritual practice and intention.

torque or torsion: A calibrated twisting of a flow of force in order to keep it at a specific rate of movement. One flow of love from the Logos is a watery torqued energy—silver. Celtic nobles wore torques, twisted silver neckbands, to signify that their wills were in service to love flowing from the Godhead. The energetic will center in the human bioenergy field is in the C7 vertebrae at the top of the spine where these torques rested.

sheaths: Each evolving form becomes encased by sheaths of varying density as it moves through its descent; the spirit is enclosed by the spirit sheath, the soul by the soul sheath, the body by the sensate sheath. These sheaths hold all memories taken in during every plane at these levels and are dissolved and reformed into light during ascension. The sheaths become a rainbow body as all fear is healed and transformed into light.

venation: Pattern of veining in leaves. The three types are palmate, pinnate, and parallel.

BOOKS OF RELATED INTEREST

BRINGERS OF THE DAWN
Teachings from the Pleiadians
by Barbara Marciniak

FAMILY OF LIGHT
Pleiadian Tales and Lessons in Living
by Barbara Marciniak

THE SACRED WORLD OF THE CELTS
An Illustrated Guide to Celtic Spirituality and Mythology
by Nigel Pennick

THE CELTS
Uncovering the Mythic and Historic Origins of Western Culture
by Jean Markale

MERLIN
Priest of Nature
by Jean Markale

TALIESIN
The Last Celtic Shaman
by John Matthews with additional material by Caitlín Matthews

KING ARTHUR AND THE GODDESS OF THE LAND
The Divine Feminine in the Mabinogion
by Caitlín Matthews

WOMEN IN CELTIC MYTH
Tales of Extraordinary Women from the Ancient Celtic Tradition
by Moyra Caldecott

Inner Traditions • Bear & Company
P.O. Box 388
Rochester, VT 05767
1–800–246–8648
www.InnerTraditions.com
Or contact your local bookseller